LONDON
PUBS

LONDON
PUBS

DAVID BRANDON

AMBERLEY

First published 2010

Amberley Publishing Plc
Cirencester Road, Chalford,
Stroud, Gloucestershire, GL6 8PE

www.amberley-books.com

British Library Cataloguing in Publication Data.
A catalogue record for this book is available from the British Library.

ISBN 978 1 84868 227 6

Typeset in 10pt on 12pt Sabon.
Typesetting and Origination by Fonthill Media.
Printed in the UK.

Contents

Introduction

The author was brought up in a generation in which the study of history at school, unless the pupil had the rare benefit of a gifted, enthusiastic teacher, was a compulsory, disagreeable and dyspeptic process, which seemed to consist exclusively of yawn-enforcing and mind-numbingly boring acts of parliament, unutterably tedious treaties, wars with all the interesting bits taken out and a seemingly endless parade of pompous, self-seeking politicians. Ordinary people, their thoughts and actions, were scarcely, if ever, mentioned. Fortunately, historical research, writing and teaching have moved on and in some circles at least, have become more demotic. This book takes an in interest in the lives of the unsung 'ordinary' people as its starting point combined with a fascination in the history of the popular drinking culture and the places where drinking took place and, of course, the ceaseless source of stimulus and wonderment that is the past and present of London. Many books have been written describing London's 'best' pubs and briefly outlining their history, associations, architecture, furnishings, fittings and facilities, but the author felt there was space for a brief, selective and non-specialist introduction to the social and cultural role that pubs have played in the life of the capital up to the First World War. Perhaps it is felt that feel that the great age of the London pub ended then.

The author hopes that the reader will accept the word 'pub' as a flag of convenience for the purposes of this introduction. Precise definitions of, and distinctions between, pubs, inns, taverns, hotels, etc need not concern us at the moment. These are not exact terms anyway but hopefully the differing general concept involved in each will become clear as we move on.

The origin of the pub is perhaps to be found in the Roman *tabernae*. These were the places in which they met to socialise and drink wine. The word *taberna* has come down into modern usage as 'tavern'. The Romans were committed to the pleasures of the grape and were less than impressed by the native preference for ale based on malted barley and often flavoured with herbs or spices. Most of the ale

A pilgrim slaking his thirst outside a primitive alehouse. He would know that ale was brewed there for sale because of the ale-stake, a forerunner of the pub sign, protruding from the front of the building.

that was consumed would have been a home brew, produced by the woman of the family (known as a 'brewster' or ale-wife). Sometimes such a brewster would gain a reputation for the quality of her ale and friends would pop in for a drink and a chat. A logical outcome was to sell ale and perhaps a corner of the hovel in which the family lived would be divided off by a primitive version of a bar. Here is the embryonic pub.

The Saxons liked their ale and developed a reputation for robust and excessive drinking for which they were condemned by the ecclesiastical authorities. The people's response was to carry on drinking with even more determination. One of the means by which the Normans imposed and maintained social and political control was through the Church. This was a major institution for almost four hundred years playing a prominent religious as well as a temporal role in English life, supporting and justifying the very inequitable nature of feudal society. Pilgrimage became big business and the monastic orders opened inns or 'guest-houses' along the routes to the shrines. Later on, as trade and commerce developed, secular inns were built along many of the major roads and in the major towns. There were many such inns in the City of London, in Southwark and along the main roads converging on London. The monasteries were dissolved in the late 1530s, but the centralising tendencies of the Tudor monarchs as well as continued economic growth meant that traffic on the roads continued to grow and provide business for increasing numbers of wayside hostelries.

The medieval inns of London would seem cheerless, austere places by today's cosseted standards. There was, as might be expected, an element of getting what you paid for. Some inns at the lower end of the market would have been crude hovels,

The southern end of London Bridge. This area and particularly Borough High Street had large numbers of inns and drinking places because many roads from southern England converged on it before making their way into the City of London.

but even at the top end, they would have been insanitary, stinking and infested with all manner of vermin. The poorer travellers might simply have lain down, preferably near the fire, on the already well-soiled rushes covering the earthen floor, and drawn their travelling cloaks around them as they tried to compose themselves for sleep. Those guests, both men and women, who could pay a little extra, might have a chamber upstairs in what was basically a dormitory. If they were lucky they might have a pallet and a straw-filled mattress. If they were less lucky it might be a large communal bed.

London as England's capital, governmental, commercial and cultural centre from medieval times always required a wide range of inns and other drinking places. Many of these offered accommodation, food and drink but also a location in which business could be transacted; deals could be done, some of them undoubtedly dirty deals; glittering intellectuals and literati (and others) could meet for more-or-less cerebral exchanges of cut-and-thrust; political plots could be woven; criminal

Some London drinking places were not for the faint-hearted.

activities could be planned and sexual seductions initiated. People met friends and socialised in pubs. Others used them simply to get drunk. In these and a host of other ways, inns and pubs and humbler establishments have played a vital part in the life of London. Foreign visitors commented on the common practice of drunken Londoners of having fun by breaking into churches and ringing the bells, making a cacophony that would wake the dead. As so often happens when people are out on a binge, it probably seemed a good idea at the time.

London was taking on an increasingly industrial and commercial character as it developed through the Middle Ages. It was overcrowded, polluted and pestilential, an ideal place for the spread of endemic and epidemic disease. Sources of fresh water became increasingly suspect and people turned to drinks based on malted barley and hops, which had been boiled in the brewing process. Strictly speaking, ale was dark, heavy and sweetish, and contained spices or herbs for flavouring. It was the traditional English beverage although preferences as far as taste was concerned varied widely across the country because the sources of the water used for brewing imparted different flavours and qualities. Beer, by contrast, was an import, brought by refugees especially from the Low Countries and who were often engaged in the woollen trade. It was lighter in colour and bitter because it contained hops, which not only gave it a more thirst-quenching quality but also contained essential oils, which helped to prolong what would now be called its shelf life. The indigenous population at first spurned beer and even attacked brewers of Flemish origin but over time the two drinks bedded down reasonably happily together with beer slowly gaining the advantage because it offered brewers and publicans various benefits over ale. Ale never left the scene completely. Our ancestors drank beer in quantities that would make most twenty-first century topers knock at the knees but much of it was 'small beer' which had a low alcoholic content and was consumed morning, noon and night by men, women and children largely to quench their thirsts. Along with bread, beer was the twin staff of life. Much stronger beer was available for 'recreational' purposes. The importance of maintaining quality in brewing and baking meant that producers who gave short measure or otherwise tried to dupe the customers were given short shrift and had to undergo humiliating public punishment.

We have said that in the early days brewing was performed as a simple domestic task but by the early fourteenth century there were signs that brewing was being carried out on a commercial basis involving an altogether larger-scale business operation whereby a brewer also owned the premises in which his products were sold. In this is the embryo of the tied-house system which dominated the pubs of London for 150 years or more.

One of the very earliest tied houses seems to have been the Bear in Southwark, first mentioned around 1320 and demolished as early as 1761, like so many since, for road-widening. It was one of London's best-known hostelries and among the attractions it offered was archery. It also had an important role as the embarkation point and landing stage for what were known as 'tilt boats', comparatively luxurious passenger vessels, which plied between London, Greenwich and Gravesend. The tied arrangement did not in this early case involve a brewer but a vintner who leased the Bear in return for which the publican agreed to buy all his wines from that vintner.

Many Londoners obtained their water supply from itinerant hucksters who always swore by the absolute purity of the water they sold – straight from a sparkling spring, they told their customers. Nothing changes there then.

The idea of making a tie-arrangement caught on more especially for beer because many publicans ran their pubs alongside other ventures, which left them with little time or inclination to brew. For the entrepreneurial brewer, possessing one or more guaranteed outlets for his products made good business sense. The term 'common brewer' evolved to describe this kind of operation.

In 1309, London possibly had 354 taverns in addition to 1,334 alehouses and a number of inns. Traditionally, taverns were somewhat superior establishments that only sold wine but they began dispensing ale as well, sometimes in an alehouse, which was part of the same premises but aimed at a lower class of clientele. Taverns were fairly rare outside of London. In 1311, in an attempt to ensure quality in the wine trade, wholesale vintners were banned from also keeping taverns so as to reduce the temptation to pour dregs back into the barrels. Another example of 'transparency', literally in this case, was the requirement that taverns had to keep their doors open so that customers could see the wine being drawn and be assured that no adulteration was taking place. Many French vintners were operating in London, their presence being the source of some resentment but their knowledge and experience put them in an unrivalled position. In 1589, the City of London was said to have had 1,000 taverns. By that time a system of licensing laid down penalties for a variety of misdemeanours. Tavern-keepers, for example, were not allowed to have guests sleeping on the premises. Over time, the differences between taverns and inns became fudged but it is no wonder that many drinking places were unlicensed in order to avoid all these niggling requirements.

In late Tudor times but especially in the seventeenth century up to the 1660s, brewing, drinking places and the drinking culture came under sustained attack from

A boisterous scene from the days of Queen Elizabeth.

those of puritan persuasion, opposed, among many other things, to the enjoyment of sensual pleasures of the bibulous sort. The politically correct brigade of their time thought, as their kind always do, that that they alone knew what was best for the human race. Such people always seem to wield more influence than their mere numbers would suggest. They influenced magistrates and therefore exercised some degree of restrictive control over brewing, drinking and drinking places. As an advance guard of the new bourgeois class that was appearing with the emergence of capitalism, their views were entirely consistent. The accumulation of capital necessary for this phase of economic development required the thrift, the diligence, seriousness and sobriety that they espoused so fiercely but which was something very alien to the majority of easy-going English working people. Popular culture right across the social strata upheld public drinking and tolerated much of the behaviour that was a consequence of drunken excess. Their efforts met with some success although by no means as much as they had hoped for.

Legislation in 1606 introduced fines or periods in the stocks for drunkenness. Its preamble pointed out that the purpose of inns and alehouses was primarily to provide hospitality for travellers and not to act as resorts for large-scale drunken dissipation. Other minor legal enactments followed. The alehouse found itself at the centre of what effectively was a class war being fought between those forces that hankered to retain the old ways of doing things on the one hand and the forces that, although they may have looked like po-faced killjoys, were actually progressive. This struggle culminated in the English Civil War and the execution of Charles I in 1649. During the period of the Commonwealth (1649-60), the puritans managed to suppress many of life's simple pleasures, including those involving drinking and the alehouse. The consequence was that most of the populace welcomed the return to the throne of Charles II because he was widely regarded as an unashamed hedonist.

It could be argued that the pubs in England in general but those of London in particular have always played a role in the often hostile interaction between the forces of authority and the will of the people. On issues such as drunkenness, gambling and Sabbath-breaking, kings and governments have repeatedly laid down decree after decree only to find that they were circumvented or otherwise rendered largely unworkable unless the populace thought they were a good idea — which wasn't very often. The pub and the culture around drinking was one of the areas in which the common people asserted a sturdy independence.

In the street called Old Bailey, EC4, stands a rebuilt and renamed pub, which used to be called the Magpie and Stump. It stood opposite the grim portals of Newgate Prison and because it had an excellent view of the spot where public executions took place from the 1780s to the late 1860s, it used to do a roaring trade on those frequent occasions on which such executions were carried out. Rooms could be rented overnight, the price depending on how good the view of the scaffold was and an 'execution breakfast' was thrown in. The price was not cheap but the devotee of hangings had overnight accommodation, a full English cooked breakfast including devilled kidneys and a grandstand view of the proceedings.

Up to 1783, those condemned prisoners who had been held in Newgate went in procession through Holborn and St Giles, and along what today is Oxford Street to Tyburn. This was close to where Marble Arch now stands. Tyburn was London's main place of execution for several centuries. A curious habit developed whereby the condemned felons were allowed some free drinks in pubs along the route. Popular prisoners were celebrities for the day and huge crowds turned out to accompany the procession or stand and cheer it on its way. Under close guard the prisoner or prisoners would be allowed a free drink and a great throng of people would accompany them, being eager to make their acquaintance on their valedictory public appearance. The Angel in St Giles High Street was one such pub. Actually basic humanity underpinned this practice because a prisoner who had had a few drinks en route to Tyburn was likely to be partially inured to the horrors of his impending fate.

Few absolutely ancient hostelries have survived in central London and the City. In the case of the latter, hundreds disappeared in the Great Fire of 1666. One miraculous survivor of the Fire is the Old Wine Shades in Martin Lane, EC4. This seems to have been almost brand new at the time and although close to where the Great Fire started, it missed the flames. It is actually a wine bar but it undoubtedly gives some of the atmosphere of an old London tavern. Some of London's oldest hostelries have been extensively renovated, yet they manage by careful contrivance to exude an air of authentic venerability. Other pubs, less ancient, are designed also to give an air of antiquity. Where it works, it is hard to know the difference. When it doesn't work, it is all too obviously phoney.

Part of the fascination of London's pubs is that not only do some of them look similar to the taverns of the seventeenth century or the ornate gin-palaces of the late nineteenth century but there is also continuity in how Londoners use them. Those who work in the financial sector still crowd into City pubs for food and refreshment in the middle of the day as they have done for centuries. Commuters still socialise in pubs after work before embarking on the journey home, pleasure-seekers continue to find a haven in the pubs of Hampstead or the riverside pubs around Kew and Richmond on sunny summer weekends and theatre-goers will still be seen flocking to the pubs of Covent Garden before taking in a show.

London is the collective term for a mass of living organisms. These consist of the City of London, the seat of government around Westminster and the coalescing of innumerable villages and districts. Some have a distinctive, historically conditioned character, while others, especially in the twentieth-century suburbs, are rather bland. As a collection of interacting organisms, London is extraordinarily complex and diverse. The whole and its component parts never stand still. Continuity and change are inseparable from the history of London. It is possible to move from a district with its own distinctive feel to another with a totally different atmosphere in the space of a few hundred yards. Affluence and poverty can be found cheek-by-jowl. Once affluent districts with grand houses can degenerate into noxious slums only to re-emerge decades later newly gentrified and with a corresponding price tag. London's pubs reflect this complicated and richly diverse history.

London has a pub licensed to sell stamps; it has another that is a licensed pawnbroker; it has pubs with theatres and boxing rings and exhibitions of oddities; it has pubs with pole-dancers; gay pubs; pubs where just about everybody is a tourist; and others heaving with politicians or lawyers or journalists. There are pubs that sell food of the highest quality and some with little more choice than salted peanuts and crisps. It still has a few spartan boozers populated by locals into which few strangers ever stray. It has tiny and intimate pubs and massive Victorian gin palaces, which represented huge financial investments when they were erected. London's pubs are as varied as London itself.

Finally by way of introduction, it should be said that London was once Britain's greatest brewing centre. This is not surprising given the population of greater London and the transport links into its extensive hinterland. In 1900, there were still about 100 common brewers in and around London, some with large estates of tied houses, others with very few. Brewing has proved to be one of the most rapacious of capitalist industries in terms of takeovers and closures, and most of London's pubs are no longer owned by brewers but by companies who view pubs as outlets of the leisure and hospitality industries. A measure of that is the fact that the only brewer of any size left in London is Fuller, Smith & Turner of Chiswick.

In the twentieth century, dozens of familiar brewing names disappeared from London's streets. Older readers may remember some of the following, which have

This large brewery once stood in Liquourpond Street, Clerkenwell. It later merged with Watney & Co.

gone since 1945. The year when brewing ceased, if known, is shown in parentheses: Reffell's of Bexley (1956); City of London Brewery, EC4; Page & Overton, Croydon (1954); North Kent Brewery, Greenwich (1965); John Lovibond & Sons, Greenwich (1959); Harman's of Uxbridge (1964); Cannon Brewery, Clerkenwell (1955); Wenlock Brewery, City Road, N1 (1962); Whitbread & Co, Chiswell Street, EC1 (1976) — they were one of the most aggressive players in the mergers and takeover game; Courage & Co, Southwark, SE1; Charrington & Co, Mile End, E1 (1975); Mann, Crossman & Paulin, Whitechapel, E1 (1979); Taylor, Walker & Co. Limehouse, E14 (1960); Truman, Hanbury, Buxton, Brick Lane, E1 (1989); and Young's, Wandsworth, SW18 (2006).

Chapter 1

London's Early Alehouses

In this section we trace the evolution of the alehouse in London from the thirteenth to the seventeenth century. Like all historical phenomena, London's drinking places have both been influenced by, and in turn had an influence on, wider economic and social developments. There is much conjuncture between the general history of London and the history of drinking and drinking places in London.

In very simple and inexact terms, inns were large establishments with a range of services, including food, drink and accommodation for well-to-do travellers. Taverns were places selling wine and possibly food to the reasonably well-heeled but not normally providing accommodation. In this hierarchy, the alehouse was the lowest element, with drink and simple food and accommodation, if any, aimed at a humbler clientele. This highly simplified structure was recognised in the growing number of legal enactments, which, over the next centuries, came to encircle the hospitality industry like creeper entwined around a trellis. The distinctions, though, were often observed in the breach.

Inns came on the scene in the twelfth and thirteenth centuries and grew steadily in numbers with the growth of London and its rising importance as the political, administrative, legal and cultural capital of England. Some became large establishments with well-appointed public rooms, comfortable accommodation, generous fare and well-trained staff. Extensive stables were needed and also storage space for goods in transit and the associated wagons and carts. In the reign of Charles II (1660-1685), we know that the Belle Sauvage on Ludgate Hill had around forty rooms and stabling for one hundred horses. Such inns were labour-intensive and the services provided were not cheap. The clientele was therefore well-to-do. Some of London's major inns hosted such events as banquets, balls, political meetings, shows and entertainments. Their customers generally being affluent and often influential, inns in this period largely avoided the legal entanglements affecting alehouses. Many business deals were transacted in inns, away from the hurly-burly of the street and other public places. Inns were centres of London life.

Taverns seem to have been in existence before inns and usually catered for those with enough money not to want to share their surroundings with others they considered as the lower orders. Taverns, at least in the early days, did not offer the range of services provided by inns and appear to have been simply drinking places selling especially Rhenish, Gascon and Malmsey wines. In 1309, it is likely that there were over 350 taverns in London.

Food was often consumed, bought in from cook-shops. Taverns rarely had any accommodation, at least they were not supposed to. As is the way of this wicked world, by the late fourteenth and in the fifteenth century, some London taverns, previously the centre of seemly behaviour, had become notorious for being places for games of chance haunted by the kind of louche characters attracted like magnets by such things. In 1393, there were complaints that certain London taverns were frequented by harlots. By the seventeenth century, some taverns were offering quite sumptuous meals. In the early eighteenth century, a meal at the Pontack's Head would have set the diner back between one and two guineas, a sizeable sum for the time. As with inns, professional people and others conducted a great deal of their business in taverns. Leading Levellers, these being political radicals, used the Nag's Head near the Guildhall as their base in the 1640s, and the Mermaid in Bread Street was noted for its eminent literary regulars. Taverns began to go out of fashion from the mid-seventeenth century finding an effective competitor in coffee-houses partly because wine had become so expensive. To survive, taverns increasingly took on the character of superior alehouses or pubs.

During the period between the thirteenth and seventeenth centuries, inns and taverns were vastly outnumbered by alehouses and they served the needs of the less well-to-do majority of the population, especially men. The alehouses themselves were very humble buildings compared to the inns and taverns. There is even less definitive information about London's early alehouses than there is about inns and taverns, probably because their users were unlikely to be among the literate minority. We know that in early times ale was brewed largely by women known as brewsters in the simple dwellings where they lived, these being the origin of alehouses and beerhouses. Some ale-wives also hawked their wares around the streets in pails or from a cask on a cart, or sold it from market stalls.

London has always done things differently from the rest of the country because of its relative size and economic weight. It was probably in London in the fourteenth century that wholesale brewers with much more highly-capitalised and sophisticated operations first appeared on the scene. The London brewers were incorporated as a livery company in 1437. By this time Flemish and Dutch brewers were producing hopped beer in London. All these brewers were selling their product to ale-houses and other retail outlets and also to other parts of the country, shipments going down the Thames and then round the coast to such ports as Bristol, Boston and Newcastle. The capitalisation of the larger London brewers allowed them some economies of scale and the trade in ale and beer was a significant contributor to the development of coastal shipping. Burton-on-Trent was one of a number of provincial centres with a reputation for their ales and its products reached London by means the Trent, the

Humber and down the east coast but not at this time in quantities to provide serious competition for the London brewers.

The origins and very early days of alehouses may be wreathed in obscurity, but it seems that from the sixteenth century, as records become more plentiful, they became the object of increasing concern and criticism from the ruling elements in society. This criticism seems to have centred on the proliferation in their numbers and the perceived threat to order that they were believed to represent. The first system of licensing was introduced in the middle of the sixteenth century and this enabled some supervision to be exercised over drinking premises. It was at this time that we first hear the argument that social problems were caused by drink and the alehouse rather than perhaps the idea that misuse of drink was a product of the economic and social tensions created within a society changing from a rural and agricultural to an urban and industrial one. Be that as it may, one writer at the turn of the seventeenth century deplored the fact that some streets in London were lined with alehouses from end to end. Perhaps he exaggerated. In 1641, there was probably one licensed drinking place in the old City for every sixteen houses, but unlicensed premises would have boosted the total. Many of both kinds of establishment, licit and illicit, besides offering drink, food and accommodation, played many other roles in the life of the community as will be seen.

Quantitative evidence on sales of beer and ale, breweries and alehouses becomes more plentiful from 1643 when excise duty was introduced on these beverages and also after 1753 when the magistrates were required by law to maintain records of all suppliers of liquor in the areas under their jurisdiction. Even though the records are unlikely to be complete, it is clear that as the population of the London area swarmed in the eighteenth century, the number of licensed premises did not keep up with this increase, which suggests stricter standards of supervision and decisive action to close down those drinking places that the licensing magistrates deemed unfit for purpose.

Sweeping generalisations about alehouses are likely at best to be half-truths. Some in the period we are looking at were little more than ill-favoured hovels with the barest minimum of furnishings and facilities but we hear of the Cock in St Martins-in-the-Fields which boasted cellars, a room for drinking with adjacent kitchen and four sleeping chambers above. Some alehouses were obviously moving upmarket! However, inventories of alehouses from the late sixteenth century suggest that most of them were still fairly humble, basically domestic premises with only the simplest items of furniture and with their drinking vessels being fashioned from cheap materials. Many of these drinking vessels were 'black jacks', which were made of wood treated with pitch inside to render them impervious and equipped with leather handles.

Operating an alehouse was not usually a passport to riches. We know that many of the more basic alehouses were run by widows and that they made just about enough money to keep themselves off poor relief, such as it was. London attracted steady inward migration from the provinces, people leaving the land for various reasons, not least because changing agricultural practices were creating unemployment. As so often happened with those who drifted to the capital, they were sadly disabused when they found that the streets were not paved with the proverbial gold. Even those with trades might be unable to use them because of restrictions exercised by the guilds and so they eked out a frugal existence keeping an alehouse. Much of the early sixteenth and first part of the seventeenth centuries were difficult times for poorer people as price inflation in various necessities caused real incomes to fall. However, the brewing of ale required only simple equipment, basic raw materials and no great skill. The most crucial factor was the cost of malt and this could fluctuate considerably, at times putting small-scale brewers out of business. Many publicans had at least one other occupation to boost their income. Occasionally a publican who had other successful strings to his bow invested money from them in his alehouse, which then gained a reputation for its superior facilities and services. He might become upwardly mobile.

Alehouses played an important role as informal labour exchanges. Particular houses would become associated with a certain trade and men coming to London looking for work would head straight for the relevant alehouse where information about vacancies would be available. In 1750, these were known as 'houses of call' and catered among others for peruke-makers, printers, carpenters, silk-weavers and hatters.

A contemporary Spanish visitor to London provides a perceptive description of the alehouse and its customers:

Alehouses... are visited by the inferior tradesmen, mechanics, journeymen, porters, coachmen, carmen, servants and others whose pockets will not reach a glass of wine. There they sit promiscuously in common dirty rooms, with large fires, and clouds of tobacco, where one that is not used to them can scarce breathe or see; but as they are a busy sort of people they seldom stay long, retuning to their several employments and are succeeded by fresh sets of people of the same rank...

By no means all the drink purveyed in an alehouse was consumed on the premises. People living nearby would fill up a container with ale and take it home. Others working close at hand would also have a takeaway, it being common for people to drink while at work, and not necessarily just those doing hard physical jobs in hot workshops and other industrial premises. The liquor sold in this way was usually small beer, drunk to quench the thirst rather than being consumed for recreational purposes. Some of the ales and beers sold for the latter purpose could be of formidable strength, intimidating by today's standards.

The English economy in the sixteenth and seventeenth centuries was changing more rapidly than ever before as it was progressing towards the Industrial Revolution. England was engaging increasingly in foreign trade, and finding herself more and more involved in a web of international economic relationships. This development, an early manifestation of globalism, meant that economic fluctuations half way across the world could have repercussions in England, leading, for example, to periods of unemployment for people who had absolutely no control over the economic forces that influenced their lives. Puritans kept banging on about idle wastrels whiling away their time drinking when they should have been out looking for work. In reality few people enjoyed enforced idleness, and the penury and pointlessness that went with it. Clearly some tried to drink their miseries

A reminder that binge-drinking is not something new.

away and this was certainly true of times when there were outbreaks of plague and various agues when ale and beer sales went up markedly, people drinking to numb their miseries and fears. One thing that puzzled the Puritans was why some people seemed to prefer drinking to eating. In fact, drink based on malted barley had considerable food value providing large quantities of calories. Beer was both food and drink, especially at a time when many water supplies were dangerous and milk was suspect.

The perception of critics at this time was that drinking and drunkenness were growing at an alarming rate — a received wisdom commonly voiced through time. If there was any truth in the assertion then the explanation may lie partly in the replacement of ale by beer. The latter was cheaper and probably had a stronger alcoholic content. Also people who drank rather than ate were likely to become intoxicated more quickly and completely. In difficult times, some people drank to gain surcease from their problems, and publicans were often prepared to extend credit to customers they knew well. More men than women drank heavily and did so drinking socially with their peer group in the alehouse rather than at home. To that extent they were away from the moderating influences of kith and kin.

Alehouses were dominated by male customers. Married women might accompany other relatives for family celebrations of various sorts — after a christening, for example. Younger women engaged in courting might accompany their swains,

Hogarth is showing the innocent country girl newly-arrived in London for the first time. She is being befriended by a 'Madam'. The odds are on that the girl will soon be lured into prostitution.

perhaps with other young couples, but otherwise women entered these premises and tarried in them to the detriment of their reputation in the community, even in a cosmopolitan society such as London's. A few might be old alcoholic drabs whose presence, if not welcome, was at least tolerated because they spent money regularly. Otherwise an unattached woman drinking in an alehouse was thought likely to be there for the purposes of prostitution and, except in some of the more disreputable houses, she was unlikely to be made welcome.

Most alehouses offered food but it would usually have been simple fare. Customers were spared crisps and other salty snacks but fried bacon, anchovies or red herrings were equally likely to encourage a lusty thirst. Otherwise bread and cheese and buns and cakes are likely to have been available. Tobacco, having been introduced to England in the 1580s, first of all attracted upper-class usage but spread to lower social groups in the early seventeenth century. It was extensively sold in alehouses. Regarded even then by some as a noxious weed, scare stories that tobacco affected the mental facilities and — for some people at least — the far more serious claim that it reduced the libido, did little to affect the spread of the new craze. Another service which alehouses provided was overnight accommodation. This was unlikely to be very grand. It was not unknown for a guest in a small alehouse to share the bed of the keeper and his wife. We are not aware whether the guest shared anything else. More commonly the guest would have had to make do with a table or rough bedding on the floor.

By virtue of their very existence as watering holes for the humbler end of the populace, Alehouses had always attracted the disapproval of those, mostly from among the better off, who thought they had the right to determine how the lower orders should comport themselves. In the late sixteenth and early seventeenth centuries, however, these prejudices were joined by growing fears that alehouses were hot-beds of political dissidence where evilly-inclined people plotted to overthrow God's ordained established order. Alehouses were already stigmatised as the resort of the work-shy and the criminally inclined, and the venue of drunken debauchees, but now additionally they were said to be places where the seeds of sedition and rebellion were being sown. Little evidence was produced to support this assertion but they led to alehouses coming under increasing pressure to be controlled and regulated more closely.

The fact is that alehouses had a myriad of different functions within the community. Those who ran them provided a vital service because they were often prepared to extend credit or act as pawnbrokers to regular customers, many of whom were hard-pressed financially. The alehouse regulars formed a valuable network of mutual community support and the easy-going sharing of drinks and chatter with convivial companions unquestionably had a bonding influence that helped to keep people going. An alehouse allowed a young man to make friends with and learn from older drinkers, and it is unlikely that this knowledge was necessarily all bad. With the sexual division of labour of the time the alehouse allowed the man of the family to escape the confines of his squalid home and what he may have thought of as the nagging wife, whose understandable bitterness with her lot gave him an ear-bashing he was keen to avoid. The alehouse took on some parts of the role in the community previously performed by the Church and was seen by the zealously religious-minded as encouraging irreligion among its users. Disgruntled prelates and priests complained that the benches in their churches were too often half-empty while the alehouses were seething with activity. Sunday, the traditional day of rest, was the alehouse's busiest day.

Certainly some alehouse keepers acted as receivers of stolen goods and were happy to allow their premises to be used by the underworld fraternity for the plotting of crime, sharing out of the booty and so on. Others allowed their customers to get too drunk as a result of which brawls and worse violence broke out, but such an alehouse keeper would probably not stay in business for long. Some alehouses were openly used by prostitutes touting for custom. An example that was basically just a brothel with beer was the Windmill and Raven in Westminster. However, it is likely that most alehouses were part of a fairly casual live-and-let-live social milieu among the common people where the self-policing of the community dealt informally with those who went beyond the bounds of what was considered acceptable.

The very rich and powerful do not at normal times feel threatened. They leave generalised insecurity to the middling sections of society who have traditionally gazed up enviously at the upper classes and looked down contemptuously on the masses, while simultaneously fearing them as well. They saw in the alehouse of the time an institution that threatened the rule of law and scurrilously promoted irreligion, idleness and insubordinate attitudes among the lower orders. Alehouses, and their lineal descendants in the public houses, were to find themselves on the receiving end of 300 or more years of increased control and regulation. The concern expressed about the evil effects of public drinking was probably exaggerated for most of this time with the possible exception of the horrors of the 'Gin Age' in the eighteenth century. Even today people vent their spleen on the subject of 'binge-drinking' when the vast majority of those who drink in a public forum do so sensibly and responsibly.

From the mid-sixteenth century onwards, the opponents of the alehouse began to marshal their efforts to deal with what they perceived as the problems posed by the existence of such places. They made less headway than they might have done since their opposition to alehouses stemmed from many different motives, which in turn meant that they could not work out an effective common strategy. Fanatical Puritans wanted all drinking places closed down. Others argued that what was needed was to maintain some well-controlled and respectable establishments by means of strict regulation of the issuing of licenses.

There was nothing new about measures to regulate alehouses. The first legal enactment on the subject was in 1495, and around 1550 a system of licensing and control, and supervision of alehouse keepers by justices of the peace was first brought in, being modified subsequently on several occasions. In 1608, as a measure ostensibly intended to raise revenue, the government required those persons licensed to run alehouses to pay a substantial annual fee for the privilege. The capital's alehouse keepers were encouraged to buy their ale from London's wholesale brewers and this gave the latter an interest to try and ensure that those retailers to whom they sold their products kept a respectable house and provided no excuse for them to be closed down by the licensing magistrates. Alehouses were not only assailed by a variety of parliamentary and quasi-governmental bodies seeking their pound of flesh and but also by their suppliers and by the various lobbies who, for whatever reason, wanted either closer supervision of alehouses or their total abolition. Modern publicans will say *'plus ça change'*.

Chapter 2

Coffee Houses

In St Michael's Alley, a narrow and easy-to-miss passage off Cornhill, EC3, is the Jamaica Wine House. A plaque on the wall explains that on this site stood London's first coffee house, opened in 1652. Within the coffee houses of the seventeenth and eighteenth centuries wide-ranging discussions and activities took place, which had an extremely important influence on English and indeed on international history. The golden age of the coffee house coincided with an explosion in scientific enquiry and learning. Coffee houses were frequented by such cognoscenti of the arts and sciences as Wren, Dryden, Reynolds, Johnson, Boyle, Swift, Gainsborough, Garrick and Hogarth. The origins of many banks and insurance companies can be traced back to men socialising and doing business in coffee houses. Such was the central role played by coffee houses in the life of London that many men-about-town were associated more with the coffee houses they frequented than with the homes in which they lived.

It is estimated that London and Westminster had at least 1,000 coffee houses in 1714. Until 1762, when such hanging signs were banned, the outside of coffee houses could usually be distinguished by a coffee pot or the turbaned head of a Turk. Dr Johnson defined a coffee house as 'A house of entertainment where coffee is sold and the guests supplied with newspapers.' So they were in their early days but, as we shall see, over the years many of them changed their modus operandi.

The first mention of coffee being consumed in Britain seems to have been in Oxford in 1637 and a coffee house apparently opened there in 1652, which may just have predated that mentioned above in St Michael's Alley. The story goes that the premises were owned by one Daniel Edwards who loved nothing better than being at home socialising and spinning a yarn with his many friends. He had a servant called Pasqua Rosee who was Turkish. He used to serve them bowls of a hot refreshing drink called coffee. This beverage had the great advantage over alcoholic drinks of allowing those taking part in these colloquies to retain their mental sharpness throughout. Indeed, the coffee even seemed to stimulate their wit and wisdom. Word got around and Edwards found he had friends he had never known before turning up on his doorstep eager to partake of his hospitality and particularly to try this exotic new drink. A bold decision was taken to go commercial and to open up the premises, selling coffee to the public.

Pasqua Rosee was put in charge of the operation. He proved to be something of a rascal. In promoting the business, he made wildly exaggerated claims about how coffee cured hangovers — a sure way of it becoming a commercial success — but he also claimed that it prevented miscarriages and could cure dropsy, gout and scurvy. According to Rosee, coffee even facilitated the breaking of aroma-free wind. Rosee's business activities meant he found it advisable to flee the country, but not before coffee-drinking caught on and his pioneering efforts had spawned a host of imitators. Coffee houses soon rivalled taverns as the focus of middle-class London social life. Some of their popularity was certainly owed to the necessity to boil the water when preparing the coffee. As London's population grew, the sources of its drinking water became ever more suspect and coffee was therefore safer to consume than water.

Coffee was one of a triumvirate of sober beverages that arrived in Britain within a couple of decades, chocolate and tea being the others. All caught on but coffee and chocolate especially became fashionable and popular at this time. The puritans initially gave guarded approval to coffee houses because they purveyed non-alcoholic drinks in respectably sober surroundings; little did they foresee that coffee would go on to become a widely-used drug.

Coffee houses were at the centre of the fervent political debates that characterised the tortured last days of the unloved Commonwealth and the arguments for and against the restoration of the monarchy. These debates gave coffee houses the reputation of being hotbeds of political activity and therefore they were viewed askance by some of the rich and powerful. The advocates of coffee houses pointed to them being a civilising influence encouraging quiet manners and decorous behaviour. Many medical men extolled the virtues of coffee as an alternative to alcohol and its various pernicious and unpleasant effects. For some, the attraction of coffee was mainly because it seemed foreign, exotic, vaguely mysterious and somehow sophisticated. Others, however, denounced coffee as an alien substance and coffee houses as the haunt of idlers, rakes and, worse than that, malcontents bent on spreading dissent and rebellion. One anti-coffee house pamphleteer wrote:

A coffee house like Noah's Ark, receives animals of every sort... a nursery for training up the smaller fry of virtuosi in confident tattling, or a cabal of kittling critics that have only learnt to spit and mew... it is an exchange where haberdashers of political small-wares meet, and mutually abuse each other and the public with bottomless stories and headless notions; the rendezvous of idle pamphlets and persons more idly employed to read them.

Another observer waxed even more splenetic about the kind of company to be found in coffee houses:

You may see a silly Fop, and a worshipful Justice, a griping Rock, a worthy Lawyer, and an errant Pickpocket, a reverend Nonconformist and a canting Mountebank; all blended together, to compose an Oglio of Impertinence.

Those who lived and worked close to coffee houses frequently complained of the obnoxious smell that assailed their nostrils when roasting was taking place. In 1657, the proprietor of the Rainbow coffee house in Fleet Street was prosecuted for creating a public nuisance while roasting his beans. Booksellers and other businesses using flammable materials felt threatened by the fire risk from nearby coffee houses. The keepers of inns, taverns and alehouses were strident in their self-interested criticism of this new form of competition. Coffee was cheaper. Seeking to make coffee an object of ridicule, even of disgust, they described it as 'syrup and soot' and 'essence of old shoes'. They were supported by a pamphleteer who around 1674 wrote 'A Satyr against Coffee' who claimed that coffee was made 'with the scent of old crusts, and shreds of leather burn'd and beaten to powder. It was the essence of old shoes, it was horse-pond liquour, witches' tipple out of dead mens' skulls, it was a foreign fart.'

The easy-going atmosphere of the coffee houses struck a chord with the collective mood of the years after the Restoration, these places providing a more suitable environment for the conducting of business or serious discussion than the frequently raucous, sometimes violent surroundings of many taverns. Some hardened drinkers found coffee houses a great boon: they used them to cure their hangovers!

The diary of Samuel Pepys, which covers almost ten years, provides a marvellous insight into London middle-class life in the 1660s. To begin with, Pepys was an unrepentant devotee of the tavern, but by 1664 visiting the coffee house had established itself as part of his daily routine. He was not overly impressed by the coffee itself but he warmed to the convivial socialising that coffee houses encouraged and the wide circle of useful contacts he could make in them. It is evident that for the man-about-town, whether working for the government, a politician, journalist, literary critic or simply the man who wanted to feel he was at the centre of things, attendance at a coffee house was time well spent.

Trade in the coffee houses suffered somewhat less than might have been expected during the Plague that ravaged London with such devastating effect in 1665. Casual patrons may have been put off by the Lord Mayor's warning of the danger of 'tippling in taverns, ale houses and coffee houses' as places where contagions might be contracted, but hard-bitten devotees of the coffee houses such as Samuel Pepys and Daniel Defoe continued to make their daily visits, taking care however not to chat with strangers. Even those they knew well would not be engaged in conversation until polite enquiries had elucidated that they and their relations and servants all appeared hale and hearty. London was, of course, traumatised by the Plague and the Great Fire that followed in 1666 but it took remarkably little time for confidence to return and with it the desire to resume the socialising and commercial activity that was associated with the coffee houses.

The rebuilding of the City after the Great Fire started almost immediately. Many coffee houses had been destroyed in the flames but it was clear that they had won the hearts of many Londoners because they were among the first buildings to arise

This was a well-known riverside coffee house-cum-tavern in Cheyne Walk, Chelsea. As well as the curiosities mentioned in the text, it displayed objects purporting to be 'the Pope's infallible candle', a purse made from a spider native to Antigua, a pair of dice used by Knights Templar and 'the flaming sword' of William the Conqueror.

out of the smouldering ruins. Over the fifty years after 1666, large numbers opened their doors for business around the Royal Exchange, Bishopsgate, Barbican and westwards to Fleet Street, the Strand, Charing Cross, Westminster and St James's, with a smattering south of the Thames in Southwark.

An early curiosity among coffee houses was Don Saltero's in Cheyne Walk, Chelsea. One of its customers was Sir Hans Sloane (1660-1753), the physician and naturalist who donated a library of 50,000 volumes and 6,000 manuscripts to form the nucleus of the British Museum. Sloane was an inveterate traveller who had accumulated a large collection of curiosities, some of which he gave the proprietor to display in his coffee house. These became well known and other patrons deposited items which added to what became a collection that drew visitors from far and wide. Some of the items may have been genuine, such as a sword that had apparently belonged to Oliver Cromwell. Less likely to pass detailed scrutiny was 'Pontius Pilate's Wife's Chambermaid's Sister's Hat'. Other items of dubious provenance included a piece of the True Cross, Mary Queen of Scots' pincushion, and a pair of nun's fishnet stockings.

The Adam coffee house in Shoreditch paid Don Saltero's the compliment of imitation. Among other items it exhibited 'teeth that grew in a fish's belly', the comb used by the biblical Abraham on the hair of Isaac and Jacob, Wat Tyler's spurs and the key purported to have been used by Adam to lock and unlock the door to the Garden of Eden.

The London coffee house allowed a respectably dressed man, after paying an inclusive admission charge of one penny, to enter well-heated premises furnished not unlike a contemporary tavern where he could smoke a long clay pipe filled with tobacco, provided by the management. He could sip a dish of coffee or some other non-alcoholic beverage, peruse the newspapers that were on hand, or listen to or partake in the general discussions that were going on. Equally he might meet others to conduct business or simply socialise. The coffee house was consciously a female-free retreat for men, the only women on the premises usually being servants. In the days of the coffee house, drinking was very much a public activity. Coffee houses, alehouses and taverns provided warmth, bustle and convivial company. To the man-about-town of those times, especially a bachelor living in what were perhaps uncomfortable lodgings, the coffee house offered a welcoming haven, which, in the early days at least, was a respectable home from home to which he could have his letters addressed and at which he could be contacted for much of the time.

Coffee houses became very important places for the circulation of news and other information. The ancestors of today's newspapers appeared in the first half of the seventeenth century. The authorities were always suspicious of printed matter especially if it disseminated political information and comment and various attempts were made to control such material. Unlicensed and therefore illegal papers were produced, but the system of government licensing of printed material lapsed in 1695 and this led to the publication of a host of newspapers, many of them being tri-weekly. The *Daily Courant* was the first daily paper, appearing in 1702. Governments continued to view such publications with suspicion and in 1715 placed a stamp duty on them. The ostensible reason was to raise tax revenue but it was hoped that the increased price would reduce demand. Stamped newspapers were indeed expensive and the coffee houses played an important role in enabling them to reach a wider readership than their circulation figures might have suggested. In the coffee houses, the day's papers were read and their contents evaluated and often vehemently argued about. The coffee house, therefore, became a natural forum in which the discussion of current affairs, the natural sciences, the classics, philosophy and the arts took place. Coffee houses helped to open access for a much wider range of people to subjects previously the exclusive reserve of such places as antiquarian societies and libraries and those few universities that existed.

It was in the coffee houses that we find the origins of the newspaper box-number system. People advertised all sorts of goods and services through the medium of a box number left at a coffee house. Illicit liaisons could be facilitated by the use of such a system, as could robberies, swindles and various other scams. Another coffee house invention was the ballot box. Sometimes a discussion would generate so much interest and controversy for and against that a vote would be taken among all those present. It was felt desirable that the voting decisions of individuals should be kept secret and so the ballot box was invented. The first time it was used was at the Turk's Head in Westminster. Tipping also began in coffee houses. Patrons began to place money in boxes marked 'T.I.P.', short for 'To Insure Promptness' — at least that's how the story goes.

Often the kind of clientele who used a particular coffee house reflected the activities that were carried on in that part of London. Lloyd's and Garraway's, for example, attracted the businessmen in the financial quarter around the Royal Exchange in the City. In Westminster, St James's and the Cocoa Tree were much frequented by politicians, the former associated with the Tories, the latter with the Whigs. Many coffee houses were situated close to St Paul's Cathedral and were patronised by clergymen and intellectuals eager to debate theological and philosophical issues. Will's Coffee House in Covent Garden, formerly a seedy drinking den called the Red Cow, was famed as the resort of London's literati. The nearby Bedford Coffee House had many glittering devotees. They included the Fielding Brothers, William Hogarth, Oliver Goldsmith and David Garrick, all eminent in their respective fields.

One of London's most famous insurance institutions traces its ancestry back to the coffee houses. Edward Lloyd owned a coffee house at No. 16, Lombard Street in the City. From around 1700, auctions of ships and of cargoes were held there and the coffee house attracted many customers involved in marine underwriting. In the congenial and informal atmosphere of Lloyd's, men of like interest met and it was but a short step for them to start conducting much of their business in the coffee house rather than on the floor of the Royal Exchange. By 1727, the business of underwriting ships and cargoes was formally moved to Lloyd's and remained there until 1771. In that year Lloyd's of London was set up, bringing together shipping underwriters from right across the City.

As London grew into the world's major banking and insurance centre, Lloyd's and other coffee houses as well as some taverns became the nuclei around which the financial institutions of the City of London developed. Important overseas trading concerns such as the East India Company and the Hudson's Bay Company all made considerable use of the coffee houses, both for formal business and for social purposes.

By no means were all of London's coffee houses devoted to the conduct of business, the shenanigans of politics or the sharpening of the intellect. England's Augustan days, which saw a flowering of achievement in philosophy, the arts and the sciences, and which coincided with the heyday of the coffee houses, were also a time of unashamedly raffish and frequently robust hedonism. There were plenty of coffee houses that were the gathering places of rakehells, cardsharpers, quacks, highwaymen, spies and scoundrels of every kind. The activities that took place in these haunts cast a shadow over the rest and probably contributed to the decline of the coffee houses.

Among men with money to spare and not infrequently among those without, gambling reached almost epidemic proportions in the eighteenth century. Certain coffee houses provided the venue in which hours were passed playing cards or other games of chance. Almost any issue provided the excuse for a bet. Men backed their fancies on the racecourse and the cricket field; they laid wagers on the size of the bag after a day's shooting; they put money on the outcome of boxing matches and cockfights; they bet on whether or not a fox would escape the hunt; on the speed at which a new cabriolet could be driven; on how soon a friend's affair with the housemaid would end, and the probability or otherwise that a child would be the result of the illicit liaison — and if it was, which sex it would be. They even staked small fortunes on which of two drips running down a pane of glass would reach the bottom first!

Many coffee houses degenerated into places of ill repute. Some coffee houses were little more than brothels or at least trysting places for clandestine liaisons and those soliciting sexual services. The rules that had been posted up for all to see in the coffee houses, the observation of which made them accepted as meeting places for 'respectable gentlemen', gradually fell into disuse. Central to the concept of the coffee house was the use of coffee as a refreshing stimulant associated with decorous behaviour. However, over time increasing numbers of them started serving alcohol and as they did so, standards of conduct rapidly declined. Many of them seamlessly transformed themselves into expensive gentlemen's clubs, while others became in effect taverns that also happened to sell coffee. One such establishment opened its doors in 1731 with the ponderous name of The London Coffee House, Punch-House, Dorchester Beer and Welsh Ale Warehouse. Given the very central role that coffee houses had played in the economic, social and cultural life of London, the decline of the institution was very rapid. Coffee, of course, continued to be consumed and has had a spectacular resurgence in recent years.

Two other relevant developments should be mentioned if only in passing. One was the 'ordinary'. This was a fixed-price set meal with a very limited choice, if any, offered on a daily basis around midday by some of London's major inns. The ordinary was usually eaten at a large communal table and beer or ale was generally taken with it. The fare consisted of a roast, perhaps a chop or two, or pies and puddings, and was food of the sort that, not altogether unkindly, used to be called 'bellytimber': a good square meal, no frills. Ordinaries had a certain vogue in the late seventeenth and the eighteenth centuries, and some of them evolved into chop

Eating and drinking have always gone together. The Ordinary usually provided a fixed-price and limited menu and was something like a chop-house and something like a pub.

houses. These proliferated particularly in the City and offered greater flexibility with food being available throughout the day and evening and they allowed small groups to sit together in boxes and booths socialising as well as eating. As the name suggests, chops featured prominently on the menu. A number of chop houses are trading to this day and some of them manage to evoke the sense of how these establishments must have looked back in the eighteenth century. The Chiswick brewers, Fullers, run a number of 'Ale and Pie' houses in Central London that could be seen as lineal descendents of the ordinaries and chop houses.

Chapter 3

Coaching Days

Coaches and coaching inns feature in framed prints found on the walls of innumerable pubs up and down the country just they also appear on Christmas cards, supposedly being redolent of the 'good old days'. In fact, much coach travel, particularly in the early days, was expensive, uncomfortable and frequently dangerous, and accommodation at the inns was often overcrowded, bug-ridden and expensive by the standards of the time. To be fair, by the time that the coaching system reached its greatest extent in the 1820s and early 1830s, coach travel had almost certainly reached the furthest limits of what was possible with horsepower. Steam-powered coaches had been tried but were not particularly successful. It was a steam-powered iron horse running on iron rails that proved to be the nemesis of the stage coach system.

A few private coaches and carriages belonging to wealthy individuals were on the roads in the sixteenth century but the progenitor of the stage coach was the stage wagon which seems to us today to be an impossibly slow and ponderous vehicle, They plied regular routes to a timetable from town to town but their prime purpose was to carry goods in smallish consignments and, if there was space, they might squeeze in one or two passengers. Because of the state of the roads before the eighteenth century, it was often quicker to walk.

The earliest stage coaches appeared around the middle of the seventeenth century. An example of a successful early service was that inaugurated in 1706 running between the Black Swan in Holborn and the inn of the same name in York. It advertised the full journey as taking four days but with the prudent proviso 'God willing'. The real spur to upgrading the stage coach system was the winning of contracts to carry the Royal Mail. In 1784, John Palmer had inaugurated an express coach connecting London and Bath. This pushed back existing perceptions of time and distance. It carried the mails and a very limited number of passengers paying premium prices and in the totally unprecedented time of sixteen hours. This was achieved because the road between Bath (then virtually the second capital of England) was of a good standard but also because the horses were changed at frequencies of less than ten miles. The coaches were heavily guarded, punctual and speedy, and they demonstrably provided a better and safer service than the slower vehicles which attracted the attention of highwaymen. The Bath service provided a model, which the more progressive concerns tried to emulate and a yardstick against which they were all judged.

As the system developed, both the cause and the result of improvements in road building and maintenance especially through the growth of the turnpike system, the coaches themselves generated much admiration and affection. However they were not without their critics. They represented the cutting edge of technology and symbolised man's determination to improve communication, not only physically but also by disseminating ideas. Coaches not only carried the mails but also conveyed printed material for which there was an increasing demand. They also transported government agents going around their business. The development of the coaching system, because it made land transport considerably easier, strengthened London's legal, administrative, political and cultural influence over the provinces. The great

The Queen's Head, Islington. When large numbers of footpads and highwaymen lurked around the roads leading into London, late travellers often stayed overnight in villages like Islington before making an early start the next morning when it was light.

Coaches were given names and here is the 'Cambridge Telegraph' at the 'White Horse' in Fetter Lane.

coaching inns of London were busy virtually twenty-four hours a day and they became major transport nodes just like their lineal descendents, the major railway termini, were to be years later. Charles Dickens captured the tone of the time in *Pickwick Papers* and it is clear not only that he admired coaches and coaching inns but that he bears much of the responsibility for the rosy image of the coaching industry that most of us have in our mind's eye. The coaching system reached its peak in the mid-1830s by which time over 3,000 stage coaches were engaged in the trade.

The City had a great many inns associated with the coaching trade and the leading ones offered services for their patrons that put them at the cutting edge of the hospitality industry. Coach travel was exhausting. Many of those who arrived at an inn in the City would perhaps just have a meal or might stay overnight before moving on elsewhere. Others with business to conduct or who were there, even in those days, seeking pleasure from being in the Metropolis, would use the inn as their base while they were in London.

In what is now Gresham Street off Aldersgate Street, EC1, stood the Swan with Two Nicks, later the Swan with Two Necks. This had much business with coaches plying to and from Bath and Bristol and the proprietor, prospering, extended his business by taking over the White Horse in Fetter Lane. His name was Chaplin and we say more about him below.

One of the best-known inns of the City was the Belle Sauvage on Ludgate Hill. It is said that it acquired this unique name as a corruption of 'Isabel Savage'. She was a sixteenth-century landlady with a good business brain who increased her turnover by utilising the galleried inner courtyard of the inn for plays and other performances and by offering such popular diversions as cock-fighting and bear-baiting. There is no hard evidence for this and other theories exist. The building probably dated back to the middle of the fifteenth century. Over the years the Belle Sauvage became one of the busiest coaching inns in the City, with services to the West of England, the Midlands, Yorkshire and Edinburgh. At one time the inn had a sign showing an aboriginal man standing by a bell. It was at the Belle Sauvage that the coachman Tony Weller, father of Sam Weller, was based in *Pickwick Papers*. The inn was demolished in 1873.

The Bull and Mouth in St Martin's-le-Grand (Aldersgate Street) was once the largest of London's inns and some idea of the business it did can be had from the fact that on a Monday, for example, twenty-one coaches left and the same number arrived. Places served included Carlisle, Glasgow, Liverpool, Manchester and Holyhead. This inn had underground stabling for no fewer than 400 horses.

This plaque commemorates the site of the Bull & Mouth Inn. This was a famous coaching inn which stood in St Martins-le-Grand. It was demolished at the end of the nineteenth century and the General Post Office was built on the site. The inn's own sign can be viewed in the Museum of London.

Other notable inns were the Spread Eagle in Gracechurch Street; the George and Blue Boar; and the Bell and Crown, Holborn; the Angel, St Clements-in-the-Strand; and the Bull, Whitechapel. The latter was the arrival and departure point for many coaches serving the eastern counties. It was a notably solid and substantial establishment and was unusual in having rooms reserved for the accommodation of the coachmen and guards where they wined and dined as sumptuously as any of the travelling guests.

Another clutch of coaching inns could be found on the south bank of the Thames along what is now Borough High Street. John Stow's *Survey of London*, published in 1598, mentions the Spur, the Christopher, the Boar's Head, the Old Pick my Toe, the White Hart and the George. Others included the Tabard and the King's Head. Since all the traffic coming to and from the City and Kent, East Sussex and the Channel Ports was channelled through this street and over London Bridge, the Borough was clearly a major traffic artery. The bridge closed at night and so belated travellers had little option but to seek accommodation in this part of Southwark. Additionally many stage wagons ended their journeys in the Borough where their goods were unloaded and stored for a day or two before being transhipped and sent across the Thames to the City. These inns were all on the east side of the High Street. Their general design was similar to those in the City in having a gateway shutting the yard off from the street, this gate being closed at night. Going through the gateway, the traveller would be confronted with a yard having three sides. It was surrounded by the inn buildings, usually of three stories and with open galleries, which gave access to the bedrooms on the upper floors and provided light. The public rooms and service facilities were on the ground floor.

The only survivor of these inns both north and south of the river is, of course, the George. Even this splendid relic has been truncated and consists of only one side of the original yard but it still manages to give some sense of how these coaching inns would have looked. The George originates from the sixteenth century and, like other inns close by also built of timber, it was badly damaged in the great fire in Southwark in 1676. The fragment to be seen today dates from about that time. Very close by is Talbot Yard where the Tabard was situated. This ancient inn probably started trading in the first decade of the fourteenth century and was immortalised by Geoffrey Chaucer as the point of departure of his motley group of pilgrims bent on journeying the road to Canterbury and paying their respects at the shrine to Thomas-a-Becket. The host at the Tabard was Henry Bailly and Chaucer uses his name and character in the tale he weaves. He is described as 'a seemly man... a merry man... bold of his speech and wise and well taught'. Chaucer's mention of this hostelry in the *Canterbury Tales* gave it almost worldwide fame:

Byfel in that seasoun on a day,
In Southwerk at the Tabard as I lay,
Ready to wenden on my pilgrimage
To Caunterbury with ful devout corage
At night was come into that hostelrie
Wel nyne and twenty in a compainye.

This inn was made famous by Chaucer as the place where the pilgrims gathered before setting off to Canterbury.

Like the George, the Tabard was destroyed in the great Southwark fire and rebuilt, re-emerging as the Talbot. For some years this inn sported a 'gallows' sign across the road — a timber beam supported by posts at either end — which made an eye-catching advertisement. In 1763, it was taken down because it was thought to be interfering with the traffic. The Talbot was demolished around 1875.

Another revered hostelry was the Golden Cross at Charing Cross which dated back before the seventeenth century. The Puritans thought its name was idolatrous and suppressed it but it reopened in happier times after the Restoration, and by the mid-eighteenth century, it was a hive of coaching activity. At its peak services departed for Brighton, a number of towns in Kent, Sussex and Hampshire, East Anglia, Gloucestershire and for Birmingham. The Golden Cross closed in 1827, the victim of town planners. A shame to see it go but at least some good came of its demolition — Trafalgar Square was built, receiving what became its world-famous name in 1835.

In London, as the coaching system developed there was probably enough competition to ensure that the major coaching inns maintained high standards and some would have been sumptuous by the criteria of the time. Coach travel was not cheap and it catered largely for those not well-off enough to own their own carriages or who did not want to travel on horseback but still had enough money to afford fares that were well beyond the pocket of the vast majority of the population. Not only were the coach fares expensive, so was the accommodation and food, and

Travellers by stage coach did not just pay the fare. Every time they stopped they were assailed by coachmen, porters and the staff of the inns, all demanding tips for services rendered or sometimes not rendered.

everyone with whom the traveller had dealings at the inns expected tips and indeed almost demanded them with menace.

The proprietors of some of the biggest coaching inns ran their own coach services. A few such men became very rich, but it was a highly competitive situation and others went to the wall. William James Chaplin was one of the successes. The centre for his activities was the Swan with Two Necks, and by 1838, he owned or part-owned 68 coaches and 1,800 horses and had over 2,000 employees. His horses pulled the coaches on their first lap out of London and their last lap into London on fourteen of the twenty-seven daily mail coaches to and from London and the provinces. Chaplin had large stables at Purley, Whetstone and Hounslow, the first stops out of London where the horses were changed along the respective routes. Hounslow enjoyed its position for two or three decades as the greatest staging post on the British coaching system, the local economy being dominated by the industry, the inns, the stables, the harness makers, the blacksmiths and the other trades ancillary to coaching. Hounslow's pre-eminence as a coaching centre ended abruptly around 1840 with the opening of the Great Western Railway. Even today, there are traces of the old coaching inns along Hounslow's High Street.

The good times enjoyed by the industry and the formidably comprehensive system of routes and services that had been built up were over by the middle of the nineteenth century.

Acceleration of the services had been taken to the limits of horsepower and one example was the Quicksilver coach that carried the overseas mails for the Falmouth packets. This left St-Martins-le-Grand in the City at 8 p.m. and reached Devonport 216 miles away at 5.14 p.m. the next day — no mean feat under the circumstances. On a fast run of that sort the horses would be changed about every ten miles. The old team could be taken off and the new one put on ready to go within a minute.

The long-distance routes were incapable of competing with the railways in terms of speed, comfort and cost, and most of the hostelries associated with the coaching trade went into rapid decline. Chaplin was astute enough to see the writing on the wall and he went into partnership with another major stage coach operator called Benjamin Horne, developing routes that fed the railways or operated to districts yet untouched by the railways. Both, with equal astuteness, eventually decided that coaching was basically finished and so they turned to buying shares in the expanding railway system and in acting as carriers and parcel agents for the railways. Although there was great affection for the coaches and their inns, within a decade or so people were equally proud of the steam trains and the great terminal stations, which played a role very similar to that which the capital's old inns had carried out.

Advanced booking was the general rule although last-minute passengers would be carried if there was space. When the ticket was issued, the passenger normally paid half the fare and the rest when he or she took up the seat. The booking clerk could not afford to make any mistakes. If he overbooked a particular journey, the coach proprietors were bound by law to convey the excess passengers by post chaise, which was much more expensive than coach travel. They then took the difference in the fares off the poor old clerk's wages!

Departures from the London inns on the long-distance services tended to be in clusters early in the morning and in the late afternoon and early evening. The earliest left around 5 a.m. in order to complete the journey on that day and the overnight coaches set out at times between 3 p.m. and 9 p.m. Examples of the routes taken were that most of the coaches for Holyhead, Glasgow, North-west England, Leeds and Hull went up Aldersgate Street and on through Barnet where the first change of horses would be made. The Edinburgh Mail went down Old Street and out of London via Shoreditch, Tottenham and Waltham Cross.

While the English were very proud of their stage coaches and of the best of the coaching inns, some of this may have been what we now call 'spin'. Benjamin Disraeli was an astute politician so he may have known all about spin. He was also a novelist of some standing, and in 1847, in *Tancred* one of his characters gives this fulsome description of dinner at a coaching inn:

> …What a Dinner! What a profusion of substantial delicacies! What mighty and iris-tinted rounds of beef! What vast and marble-veined ribs! What gelatinous veal pies! What a colossal ham! Those are evidently prize cheeses! And how invigorating is the perfume of those various and variegated pickles!…'Tis a wondrous sight.

William Chaplin was one of the most successful inn-keepers who expanded into the coaching industry.

This famous ancient coaching inn stood in Tothill Street, Westminster.

This once prosperous coaching inn has closed and degenerated into slum housing and a place for storage. The Oxford Arms stood in Warwick Lane, EC4. The picture was taken about 1870.

We think of a the Elephant & Castle as one of those road hubs that never goes to sleep but this impression of it dated around 1780 shows that it was quite busy in those days too.

Such a paean of praise was, however, wasted because the new-fangled railways carried all before them. The period from the mid-1830s to the 1880s saw the continuous rise of the railways during which time London found itself the focus of a railway network of baffling complexity. Hostelries, which predated the railway, suddenly found that overnight they were dragged out of relative obscurity when they gave their names to railway stations and subsequently to the district in which they were located. The Angel, Islington; Bricklayers Arms, Bermondsey; Elephant & Castle, Newington and Royal Oak near Paddington are examples. Later on, bus and tram termini were frequently located at pubs and the Archway Tavern and the Swiss Cottage have given their names to their respective surrounding districts.

Although inns were supposed to be distinguished by the fact that they provided accommodation, no matter how basic, and operated under a different licensing system, over the centuries these distinctions became fudged and there are to this day hostelries whose names include the word 'inn' but which do not and never have offered accommodation.

The heyday of the coaching inns was a brief but glorious one.

Chapter 4

Taverns

James Boswell in his entertaining biography of his great friend Dr Johnson declared:

> There is no private house in which people can enjoy themselves so well as at a capital tavern... there is nothing which has yet been contrived by man by which so much happiness is produced, as by a good tavern or inn.

The heyday of the tavern was roughly from the 1560s to the 1780s, a time when wine was cheap. Taverns carved out a unique and crucial role in the life of London during that period. Taverns were manifestly urban phenomena and although some provincial towns such as Bristol and Norwich could boast a few, it was with London and particularly the City that they were most associated. They were the places where the 'movers and shakers' of the day went to enjoy themselves. The customers were predominantly male, of middling wealth and social status. Many were intellectuals — cognoscenti and literati, people from the arts, sparkling wits and those who merely thought they were, the legal profession, MPs, bankers and merchants, physicians and government bureaucrats, rakes, scoundrels and confidence-tricksters, bucks and beaux. On the fringe was the inevitable collection of toadies, lickspittles and place-seekers.

These people went to taverns for any number of different reasons but what united them was their consumption of wine. Many of them took wine in quantities almost incomprehensible to the modern mind but it must be remembered that for large sections of seventeenth and especially eighteenth-century society, there was no stigma attached, either to consuming copious amounts of drink in public, nor to being very drunk in public. Many of the leading political, professional and intellectual figures of their times frequented taverns where they regularly became immoderately drunk and then proceeded to work. Some were more-or-less permanently drunk. Politicians

A contemporary depiction of a Tudor tavern scene.

frequently made speeches and conducted parliamentary business when they were clearly in their cups. It is a wonder that the literati ever managed to string more than a sentence or two together for posterity given the time they spent tarrying in taverns. Drinking wine was a mark of social class and exclusivity. Taverns had a virtual monopoly of selling wine, and so those who resorted to taverns did so in order to do business, to 'network' or just to relax and enjoy themselves among others of their own sort. Among London's classic taverns were the Mitre in Cheapside, the Spiller's Head in Clare Market, the Devil at Temple Bar, the Falcon at Bankside and the Star & Garter in Pall Mall.

If there is one great Londoner associated with taverns, it has to be Dr Samuel Johnson (1709-84). Strictly-speaking he was only an adopted Londoner but it was in the metropolis that he found fame and carved out the lifestyle that clearly gave him such enormous pleasure. Let him give his opinion of what the tavern had to offer:

> As soon as I enter the door of a tavern, I experience an oblivion of care, and a freedom from solicitude; when I am seated, I find the master courteous and the servants obsequious to my call, anxious to know and ready to supply my wants; wine there exhilarates my spirits and prompts me to free conversation, and an interchange of discourse with those whom I must love; I dogmatise and am contradicted; and in this conflict of opinions and sentiments I find delight.

One little-known aspect of London's taverns is that many of them issued tokens in the middle of the sixteenth century. There was a chronic shortage of small coinage, which was hampering the businesses of many shopkeepers. To circumvent this, many traders, including tavern-keepers, started issuing their own unofficial and illegal tokens to which the government sensibly turned a blind eye. Three thousand trade tokens were issued just in London and almost a thousand of these were tavern tokens. These tokens usually showed the sign of the inn and the name of the issuer on the obverse side while on the reverse were displayed the initials of the tavern-keeper and his wife and the address of their premises. These tokens had a limited circulation in the locality of the taverns concerned among those who felt assured about the probity of the issuers.

Taverns went out of fashion from the middle of the eighteenth century. The new up-and-coming section of the bourgeoisie consisted on men of a very different kidney from the tavern habitués of the two centuries before. Now it was 'new money' that was beginning to call the shots. Some of these were horny-handed self-made men. Whatever their social origins, the inventors, scientists, industrialists, factory-owners, traders and entrepreneurs who contributed to the Industrial Revolution were not the kind of men for whom lounging around taverns for hours in a semi-drunken state engaging in metaphysical discussion had any attraction. The taverns found their ambience being copied by some of the more up-and-coming alehouses and they increasingly lost their former devotees to these, to coffee-houses and to the emerging gentlemen's clubs, all of which took to selling wine and to which indeed some of them actually converted.

The Boar's Head in Eastcheap, EC3, was a notable example of a City tavern. It was an ancient establishment first mentioned towards the end of the fourteenth century and it was destroyed in the Great Fire. Soon after the Fire it was rebuilt and it gained some fame when many years later its sign was recovered from a mound of rubbish in Whitechapel after the tavern itself had been demolished in the 1780s. It was a carved boxwood bas-relief boar's head in a circular frame formed by two boars' tusks. Even then it was regarded as a collector's item and it was bought and sold many times over the following centuries before eventually ending up, not quite intact, in the Museum of London. This sign is dated 1566, exactly a century before the Fire. The tavern is mentioned by Shakespeare and it also provides

An interior view.

evidence of its continued existence with a number of farthing tokens issued by the landlord in the middle of the seventeenth century. It became the venue for an annual Shakespeare banquet, the last of which took place in 1784 and at which members of a Shakespeare Club donned the costume of various characters from the Great Bard's plays. Other notable former taverns included the Barley Mow, Salisbury Square, EC4, and the Crown and Anchor in the Strand. Among the regulars at the latter were Dr Johnson and Sir Joshua Reynolds. It was a favourite meeting place of politicians and in 1798 hosted a monster banquet in honour of Charles James Fox with the Duke of Norfolk in the chair. It burnt down in 1854. The Half Moon in Aldersgate Street, E1, stood on the site of the present Half Moon Passage. This achieved minor fame because Ben Jonson was a regular but he made his way there on one occasion only to find it closed. Disappointed but not put out, he went to the Sun in Long Lane instead and penned off a quick verse, something he was very good at doing. It went:

Since the Half Moon is so unkind,
To make me go about,
The Sun my money now shall have,
And the Moon shall go without.

The tavern most visited by the ubiquitous Dr Johnson was the Mitre in Fleet Street. Although this probably dated back to medieval times, it is first mentioned in 1603 when the authorities complained that a door from the tavern allowed fugitives from the law to make their escape into the warren of dangerous alleys and courtyards which made up the criminal rookery known as 'Alsatia'. Once there, the fugitive had virtual immunity from the forces of law and order. Pepys was one of the regulars, while it was in the Mitre in 1763 that Dr Johnson made his famous cutting retort to the Scotsman who was extolling the virtues of his country. What Johnson said was, 'Sir, let me tell you, the noblest prospect which a Scotchman ever sees, is the high road that leads him to England.' The tavern closed in 1788, and the building was demolished in 1829.

It is unfortunate that we have little choice but to accept the terminological inexactitude concerning taverns, inns, pubs and the rest. However, if we start by accepting the concept of the tavern outlined above in this chapter then a strong claim could be made that Ye Olde Cheshire Cheese in Wine Office Court off Fleet street, EC4, currently provides the best evocation of how the taverns of old times must have looked. It is likely that there has been a drinking place on this site since about 1539. This building was at least partly destroyed in the Great Fire but was quickly rebuilt if the lamps outside, which say '1667', are anything to go by. Internally it is a warren of small rooms, corridors and ancient staircases with much blackened oak panelling and open coal fires to warm the cockles of the heart in cold weather. Until recently there was sawdust on the floors. Under part of the pub are vaulted cellars thought to have been part of a thirteenth-century Carmelite monastery that once occupied the site. To the right of the understated main door is a list of English monarchs who have reigned during the life of the 'Cheese'. The whole place is attractively understated.

One literary figure we do not know for absolute certainty drank and held forth here is, strangely enough, Dr Johnson. While there is no actual proof that he used the 'Cheese', it is hard to think that he didn't given that he lived close by for many years. A chair is displayed with the proud boast that he placed his ample posterior on it, but some cynics say that while Johnson may indeed have sat on this chair, it is actually from another tavern not far away. Other literary figures, men of the arts and intellectuals who certainly whiled away the hours in the 'Cheese' include Oliver Goldsmith, Thackeray, Arthur Conan Doyle, Joshua Reynolds, David Garrick, Hood, Cruikshank, Wilkie Collins, Mark Twain, Dickens, Chesterton and W. B. Yeats, although not all, of course, at the same time. Given the amount of time such people seem to have spent engaged in the cut-and-thrust of rapier-like repartee, it is a wonder that any of them ever got round to putting pen to paper or paint on canvas.

The poet John Davidson (1857-1909) who sadly committed suicide by drowning had clearly, in happier times, appreciated the charms of the 'Cheese'. Here are some excerpts from lines he wrote in its honour:

I knew a house of antique ease
Within the city's smoky pale,
A spot wherein the spirit sees
Old London through a thinner veil.
The modern world so stiff and stale,
You leave behind you when you please,

For long clay pipes and great old ale
And beefsteaks in the 'Cheshire Cheese'.

If doubts or debts thy soul assail,
If Fashion's form its current freeze,
Try a long pipe, a glass of ale,
And supper at the 'Cheshire Cheese'.

For decades the 'Cheese' was renowned for its puddings. By any standards, these were large, weighing between 50 lbs and 80 lbs. Within a light pastry crust was a mixture containing beefsteaks, kidneys, oysters, larks, mushrooms, spices and gravy, all to a secret recipe. This monster pudding took sixteen to twenty hours to cook and its appetising aroma is said to have titillated nostrils as far away as the Stock Exchange. The pudding season started on the first Monday in October and a distinguished public figure would be invited to make a ceremonial first cut. Several Prime Ministers and other politicians, bishops and literary men have done so, and even Jack Dempsey (1895-1983) was prevailed upon to do so. Dempsey was the American heavyweight boxer whose chilling nickname was 'The Manessa Mauler'.

Perhaps even more formidable in its own way than Jack Dempsey, was Polly, the immortal talking parrot of the 'Cheese'. This parrot was presented as a gift to the then landlord by a sailor who had trained it well. Its vocabulary was extensive and mostly profane and it was an absolute master of foul-mouthed invective. It also possessed a superb sense of timing and an unerring memory for faces. Regulars would merely be greeted with a sardonic snort or a sarcastic aside but it was on strangers that Polly really enjoyed exercising her splenetic vocal chords. She would launch into a flood of verbal filth so forceful and merciless that strong men were known to have blanched, blushed and beaten a hasty retreat, swearing they would never return. But return they mostly did because Polly was good for trade. People who had never visited London before made a beeline for the 'Cheese', eager to hear Polly in action. Another party trick was an extraordinarily lifelike impression of a cork being withdrawn from a bottle and the convivial glug-glugging sound of wine being decanted. Polly was no respecter of social rank or class and, when she was in the mood, she happily foul-mouthed all-comers including Queen Mary to whom she was presented in 1922. Polly contracted pneumonia and died in 1926. Her obituary appeared in newspapers printed as far away as Australia and the USA. Polly was irreplaceable. No parrot even tried.

The word 'tavern' has been included in the name of many later drinking places that by any definition cannot actually be regarded as taverns. An example of a place that was a pub plain and simple but which had the official name the Railway Tavern was Charlie Brown's in West India Dock Road, E14. This was a legendary dockside boozer made famous by its landlord Charlie Brown (1859-1932) who was born locally and went by the nicknames of 'Uncrowned King of Limehouse' and 'Squire of the Manor of the West India Dock Road'. Gaining little formal education, he ran away to sea as a youth. This experience was one he did not enjoy so he came back and worked in a bakery until becoming a publican at the Duke of Cambridge in Whitechapel Road. This was where he started to accumulate a collection of curios and when he took on the Railway Tavern, he brought them with him. This was

Examples of tokens worth one half-penny issued
by the 'Pageant Tavern' at Charing Cross.

about 1896 after which the collection simply grew and grew until much of the
pub was given over to space in which these exhibits could be viewed. Contrary
to common belief, this high-class bric-a-brac was not donated to him by sailors
from ships in the docks but was the result of his own assiduous collecting and
arrangements with agents overseas who bought on his behalf. Many of the items
were composed of ivory and were valuable. Some were very large and people
came literally from the four corners of the earth to view them. No admission
was charged but donations were encouraged and distributed to local charities.
Huge sums were raised over the years that Charlie Brown was the 'Guv'nor'.
During the 1912 dock strike he raised large amounts of money to help the
strike fund, and he went on to act as the honorary treasurer of the Stevedores'
Union. When he died, he lay in state in the pub and thousands filed past to pay
their respects, and a massive funeral cortege made its way to Bow Cemetery
through streets lined several people deep. There were 140 floral tributes. The
pub was demolished in 1989 when the area was being redeveloped and was
changing out of all recognition, not necessarily for the better.

The definition of a 'tavern' is not exact, but it can be seen that taverns have
played an honourable role in London's history.

Chapter 5

The Gin-Drinking Scourge

Early in the seventeenth century, a studious professor of medicine at the University of Leiden was busy researching to find a cure for various virulent fevers affecting settlers in the Dutch colonies. Among concoctions he experimented with was one combining alcohol and juniper berries. It proved highly efficacious. It didn't do much to cure the fevers but it made the patients feel a whole lot better! Thus was born — if the story is true — 'genever' or gin, a spirituous liquor which Dutch distillers then began manufacturing and exporting profitably around Europe. Its medical potential was quietly forgotten as it proved a great hit particularly in England and nowhere more so than in London.

Londoners were no strangers to spirits, not only consuming French brandy and Irish whisky but also the produce of local distillers who in 1638 received permission from Charles I to become the Worshipful Company of Distillers with a monopoly of distilling in the London area. It was felt that the health risks that even then were known to be associated with the excessive consumption of spirits could best be kept within acceptable bounds by having some control over distillers. William and Mary came to the throne in 1689 and promptly dissolved the Worshipful Company of Distillers' monopoly. They now decreed that just about anybody could start operating as a distiller. William, a staunch Protestant, harboured an absolute hatred of Catholic France and this action was intended to reduce the amount of French brandy being consumed in England. The landowning class, dominant in Parliament, were very keen on the measure because they would benefit from the enhanced consumption of indigenous grain, especially barley, used as a raw material for gin.

Gin production burgeoned particularly in London and each distiller tried to create a distinctive product by using fruits or herbs and thereby developing a brand with a unique flavour, in particular one that masked the spirit's essential acerbity. Dutch gin and many of the different indigenous gins produced at first were of formidable strength but at least they were pure. Soon, get-rich-quick producers appeared on the scene and adulterated the gin they sold with a variety of debased ingredients, possibly up to and including sulphuric acid. A price war broke out and gin, especially at the lower end of the market, became extraordinarily cheap. It cost little and was warming but also addictive and poisonous. Drinking gin had at first been seen as something patriotic and Protestant, a slap in the face for foreigners and Catholics, but it quickly came to be regarded as a cheap and easy way to get extremely drunk. The hangovers were horrendous. The best cure was another drink.

The consequence was gin drinking of almost epidemic proportions. Sales of ale and beer in London continued to be buoyant, but many drinkers, especially those who were the most desperate to obtain temporary relief from their miseries, gleefully and gratefully poured cheap gin down their throats. In 1684 about 530,000 gallons of gin were being consumed. In 1751, in London alone, over eleven million gallons of gin were consumed. Not only did business boom for the large-scale distillers but tens of thousands of 'back street' producers also got in on the act. A quarter pint of a rotgut concoction of formidable alcoholic strength masquerading as gin could be bought for just 1d. Oblivion followed quickly as indeed, on occasions, did death.

The poor of eighteenth-century London lived in squalid hovels, working, when they could find employment, for poverty wages. Their life expectancy was markedly less than that of the rural poor as they suffered from a range of contagious diseases, which prospered in the foetid, ill-ventilated, overcrowded slums. Other physical conditions endemic to their poverty and surroundings took their toll in an era when the concept of public health had not been invented. Filth, much of it the source of disease, was everywhere and with vast quantities of sea-coal being burned, the atmosphere was acrid and choking and could be lethal for those with respiratory problems.

Gin, therefore, was a quick fix, which provided effective surcease from the misery that was the constant lot of most of London's poor. Gin literally took over the lives of many Londoners — men, women and even children. When they were awake it debilitated their will to work or do anything positive with their lives, and because gin was so cheap, lots of people were more-or-less permanently drunk. A little casual crime would obtain the few pennies needed for more gin and another escape from reality. Many custodians of drinking places were happy to allow their patrons to drink themselves into insensibility, allow them to sleep on straw on the floor and then ply them with more gin when they woke up. But gin did not necessarily make for blissful oblivion. Many drinkers became quarrelsome and violent. The London rich have always lived in fear of what they think of as the 'swinish multitude'. London was famous for its mobs, and they were even more threatening when they were drunk.

The evident economic and moral decay brought about by the abuse of gin forced the government to take rather half-hearted action with the Gin Act of 1729. This increased the duty on gin and required those selling it to obtain a license. It was prohibited to sell gin on the streets. Many retailers of the liquid filth called gin simply circumvented the act by giving their products other names. The act was unpopular, impossible to enforce and was repealed in 1733. Many MPs were torn between their interests as landowners wanting to keep up the demand for homegrown grain and their concern that the economic, commercial and industrial life of London was literally being threatened by the gin-drinking craze. A drunken mob took to the streets in an orgy of violence and destruction on the eve of the act becoming law. The act sought to reduce the number of distillers and control them more effectively and introduce more severe punishment for infringement of the law. In practice, the 1736 Gin Act proved to be hardly more effective than the previous legislation. Londoners were now addicted to gin and were going to obtain it one way or another. Illicit distillers and large-scale smuggling of gin more than compensated for the effects of the act, while some retailers got round the law by selling gin with labels suggesting, for example, that it was a medication. Many of those who were in employment happily received part of their wages in the form of gin.

The new law did little to prevent vast numbers of Londoners, most especially the poor, seeking escape from the miserable lives by means of 'Mother Gin'. While the addiction to gin may have brought temporary oblivion, it was a joyless escape from reality and came with a heavy pricetag. Drunken nursing mothers unwittingly sowed the seeds of their offspring's future alcohol dependency as they gave suck; thousands became ill or died prematurely of liver and other diseases; drunken, often entirely promiscuous, sexual couplings failed (perhaps thankfully) to lead to conception as the habitués of gin became infertile. Jailers ran a profitable sideline selling gin to those of their inmates who could afford to buy. People in an almost permanent gin-induced stupor were totally incapable of purposive behaviour. Many would take a dram or two of gin rather than eat; gin staved off the pangs of hunger. Magistrates attested to the fact that large numbers of the wretches who appeared before the bench were there accused of drink-related offences, usually theft and violence. Gin was blamed for just about every kind of crime and example of civil disorder.

There was much migration into London in the first half of the eighteenth century but despite that the population actually declined and the blame for that can almost certainly be laid on the gin-drinking mania. The figure of over eleven million gallons of gin consumed in London in 1751 gives an extraordinary average annual consumption per head of the population of almost sixteen gallons. A survey of London in 1739 stated that London had a total of 95,968 houses of which 15,288 sold alcohol for consumption on the premises. Gin was also sold from market stalls, from barrows wheeled by itinerant hucksters and from a wide range of shop premises. Some of these 'gin-shops' were simply domestic premises, which were unlicensed and of which no records have survived. Many pubs sold gin perfectly legally but were little more than brothels in which prostitutes found it easy to rip off and rob the punters. Even some Thames watermen sold gin to those who used their services as water-taxis. Gin sellers did a roaring trade at public hangings, and Hogarth depicted a gin seller in his *The Idle Prentice Executed at Tyburn* (1747).

William Hogarth (1697-1764) encapsulated his opinion of the degradation, despair and debauchery that accompanied the abuse of gin in *Gin Lane*, which, along with *Beer Street*, is perhaps the best known of all his prints, and it is where he expresses his moral indignation with great artistic genius. This was art as propaganda. *Gin Lane* is a direct attack on gin drinking and its associated evils. The scene is recognisable as St Giles', one of the worst criminal rookeries in London, where every fourth house was said to be a gin shop. Steps lead down to a cellar

William Hogarth's biting satire on the misery caused by the abuse of gin.

above the doorway of which is the inscription 'Drunk for a Penny, Dead drunk for two pence, Clean straw for nothing.' A cadaverous-looking figure in the right-hand corner is holding an empty glass and represents a well-known street-seller whose cry was 'Buy my ballads and I'll give you a glass of gin for nothing.' About the only person prospering is the pawnbroker where a carpenter can be seen pledging his saw to obtain the money for a drink, while a woman is about to pledge a collection of pots and pans for the same purpose. An ulcerated and otherwise squalid-looking woman, a parody on the Madonna, is in a drunken stupor and allows the infant she has been suckling to fall head first into the alley below. A barber, ruined by drink, can be seen having hanged himself from a beam, while a drunken madman has impaled a child on a stake. A child is lying on the ground, while its dead gin-soaked mother is taken away in a coffin.

By contrast, Hogarth makes 'Beer Street' glorify the robust and wholesome pleasures associated with England's national drink and he depicts a scene of contentment and jollity. Here all is prosperous and thriving with the conspicuous exception of the pawnbroker's. He can be seen reaching out of a wicket door for a tankard of porter, not daring to open the door fully for fear that his creditors will gain entrance. On the left, two portly men, one a butcher and the other a blacksmith, are contentedly holding foaming tankards of best English bitter. An amorously-inclined drayman is busily chatting up a servant girl. The pub is doing well and is employing a happy-looking painter up a ladder working on a new signboard.

Alcohol was part of the fabric of eighteenth century life for all classes but the rich could afford a wider variety and greater quality in the potations they consumed. Drunkenness per se was not regarded as a vice, and writers like Daniel Defoe referred with pride to the ability of doughty natives to put away many pints of honest ale. Many of the beers of the seventeenth and eighteenth centuries were formidably strong but they were nutritious in a way that gin absolutely was not. Some gins were so adulterated or debased that they were little more than dangerous poisons, lethal in some cases. One recipe for a proprietary gin numbered among its ingredients vitriol, turpentine, alum and salt of tartar. Beer and ale were the traditional beverages of the poor and ones with a low original gravity were drunk to quench the thirst at a time when water supplies were often seriously polluted. Certainly many people quaffed stronger beers and ales in order to become inebriated but the supping of gin had an almost instantaneous effect and was more appealing to those who wanted a quick escape from reality. 'Quaffing' is not exactly a word normally associated with the drinking of spirits but that is precisely what some desperadoes did and there were many reports of people downing a pint of gin in one draught, or drinking two or more pints very quickly and then literally dropping down dead. A sudden, sizeable infusion of neat gin into an empty stomach could be lethal.

The production of alcoholic drinks provided considerable employment and their consumption raised valuable tax revenue, not least to finance the apparently endless wars with France in the eighteenth century and the military and naval campaigns involved in acquiring an empire. In government circles there was at this time little or no opposition to drinking as such. Many leading political figures spent much of their waking time more-or-less drunk. Their concern about and opposition to gin drinking was on the grounds that it corrupted the morals and the working

Gin killed thousands in the eighteenth century and undermined the will of tens of thousands of others to do anything about their wretched existences.

habits of the poor. The rich had (and still have) a view of morality in which they saw themselves and the poor being governed by very different sets of behavioural precepts. Gin consumption was seen as insidiously undermining the obedience and deference owed by the lower orders to their betters. Criticism of gin drinking from the rich was part of their ongoing crusade to mould and control the morals and behaviour of the poor. In fact the root cause of the gin craze was generalised poverty and the miseries that it brought in its wake, not moral turpitude. That was something the rich could not or would not ever understand. Many of the legislative attempts to control the gin 'problem' were aimed at the part-time working-class dealers for whom the chance to make a few pennies on the side could mean the difference between a meal on the table and going hungry. Money was even available as a reward for 'snitches', other working-class people who would inform the authorities when they found evidence of peers who were illegally engaged in selling gin without the requisite license.

When attacks were made on excessive drinking and the vices, which supposedly followed inevitably in its wake, no one pointed an opprobrious finger at strong ales and beers. Indeed consumption of these remained buoyant throughout the eighteenth century. Some opponents of gin went so far as to argue that workers who consumed beer were able to work faster and better. Some opposition to gin-drinking was on sexist grounds; generally speaking, men in jobs that were particularly physically demanding, and there were huge numbers of these among London's teeming industries, stuck to beer as being more refreshing and better for replacing

It is unlikely that hangovers have changed much down the centuries.

moisture that had been sweated out. Gin was more likely to be consumed by men in the sedentary occupations and by women. As ever, women drinkers were seen as a threat. Gin-sodden women were bad wives and mothers, predatory and pox-ridden whores and probably infertile to boot. Women who drank were seen as threatening the social order. Several prominent brewers sat as MPs and they formed a small but powerful pro-beer and anti-gin lobby, making the most of this maelstrom of pseudo-moralistic posturing. The temperance movement, the efforts of which were to bedevil the world of brewing and distilling in following centuries, was, however, scarcely a factor in the eighteenth century.

Concerns about the effects of gin drinking had been expressed early in the eighteenth century and were manifested in acts of parliament in 1729, 1736, 1743 and 1751. The first three were widely circumvented. The act of 1751 was rather more effective in restraining gin-drinking, partly by increasing its price, but it was repeated crop failures from 1757 that forced the government to restrict the use of home-raised grain for distilling and which brought about a fall in gin consumption to the figures that had pertained around 1720. In 1750, in Westminster, there had been 1,300 licensed retailers and about 900 who were unlicensed; in 1794, there were 'only' 957 retailers and all were licensed. In 1797, all tax restrictions were lifted from the brewing industry and the great days of gin were most definitely over.

A persistent opponent of gin was the Revd James Townley. On occasions he pursued his anti-gin campaign through verse. Here is an example:

Gin! Cursed fiend with fury fraught,
Makes human race a prey,
It enters by a deadly draught,
And steals our life away.

Virtue and truth, driven to despair,
In rages compels to fly,
But cherishes with hellish care,
Theft, murder, perjury.

Damn'd cup that on the vitals preys,
That liquid fire contains,
Which madness to the heart conveys,
And rolls it through the veins.

Beer! Happy produce of our isle,
Can sinewy strength impart,
And wearied with fatigue and toil,
Can cheer each manly heart.

Chapter 6

The Swan Song of the Alehouse

Londoners had been drinking in alehouses for centuries. These establishments had evolved little during that time and at the beginning of the eighteenth century, virtually all of them were still domestic premises adapted for the purpose of hospitality. They were simple places, usually consisting of just one public room, which was often referred to as the 'parlour', thereby revealing their domestic origins. The rest of the building was the domicile of the alehouse keeper and his or her family. Some sold groceries and other necessities, although less so with the increase in fixed shops, and many provided food and accommodation, in both cases of rather a rudimentary character. Brewing on the premises was steadily being replaced by the buying in of drink from wholesale brewers. Some alehouses had been bought by these brewers and were tied to selling their products. Alehouses carved out a varied and vital role for themselves in the community but they were probably taken for granted by their customers who were largely male and who tended to be down the lower end of the social scale. In fact, this century was to be their swan song and, in London at least, by 1800 they were being rapidly supplanted by other types of drinking place.

With growing capitalisation and commercialisation of brewing, the humble alehouse was increasingly being supplanted by the 'public house'. This was an establishment occasionally adapted from an existing building but often specifically designed for the purpose of selling alcoholic drinks. They differed enormously in size and the public house generally contained several rooms each serving different functions and aimed at a different clientele. These rooms were often graded in terms of furnishings and comfort. In the case of the best rooms, customers usually paid extra for their drinks in order to enjoy some social exclusivity. They might also be served at their tables. The public house represented a considerable investment of capital and the brewers who owned them were determined to maximise the return on that investment. Many of these 'common brewers' as they were known became rich and powerful, and rose to take their place in the City 'establishment' and some also entered Parliament where they formed a powerful lobby.

In the eighteenth century, Britain was becoming an increasingly industrial and urbanised society, which had widespread social, political and cultural effects. Drink and the culture around it became increasingly industrialised, commercialised, controlled and regulated. The rich classes had a great fear of the urban working class, particularly in London where the so-called 'mob' had a history of volatility, violence and lack of deference towards its supposed social superiors. Industrialisation required a regular disciplined workforce putting behind it the casual ways associated with pre-industrial employment patterns. Attitudes of sobriety and diligence were required and these did not sit easily with the traditional noisy, bawdy and drunken leisure pursuits of the masses. In this situation a kind of bifurcation of drinking places occurred. Many tried to create the facilities, furnishings, fittings and general ambience that would attract those looking to enjoy a drink in moderation and in reasonably decorous surroundings. Others unashamedly geared their provision to the lower end of the market. This was the way that some alehouses chose to go and they gravitated to the murky world also inhabited by beer shops and large numbers of seedy and frequently sinister dives, often illicit, selling mostly low grade gin and other cheap rotgut spirits such as brandy.

From the time of the gin craze, 'respectable society', and not just its more puritanically-inclined elements, came to see drinking as a problem that needed to be addressed by politicians and the law because otherwise it might spin out of control. However, what was often not understood was that if drinking was such a problem it was not because of innate human wickedness but largely because of the dirt, deprivation and despair that was the everyday lot of hundreds of thousands of Londoners at the lower end of the social scale.

As governments kept increasing tax on beer, partly to raise revenue but also, paradoxically, to deter excessive drinking, London drinkers exercised some ingenuity and began asking for 'three-threads'. This was an attempt to get the strongest drink for the lowest price. It involved mixing three brews, one strong and expensive and the other two weaker and tasting very different. This was a nightmare for the pot-boys who, in fetching the drink to the customer, obviously had to draw beer from three barrels, which enormously increased their workload.

A major development in the eighteenth century was the emergence of porter brewing in the 1720s. Porter was the brewer's dream. Although it needed heavy initial investment, once the necessary equipment was up and running, porter was relatively cheap to produce and retail, and easy to handle and store in large quantities. This gave the brewers economies of scale and high profit margins, and it led to what is euphemistically called 'consolidation' in the industry whereby those concerns that could afford to invest in the production of porter stole a march over their smaller rivals who went to the wall. In 1748, the twelve biggest London brewers were responsible for 40 per cent of the beer being produced in the capital and it is no coincidence that all of them included the brewing of porter in their portfolios. With the profit margins they were enjoying, especially from the brewing of porter, they set about buying up alehouses to create a tied estate of outlets for their products. Many smaller breweries collapsed, and brewing on the premises by alehouse keepers was dying out.

Many pubs in London used to advertise 'entire'. This was a new brew which appeared in the eighteenth century and had the characteristics of mild ale, bitter and strong beer.

Porter was a heavy, black, bitter-tasting drink and arguably got its name from its popularity with the porters in London's many wholesale markets. 'Stout' was a stronger, more expensive version. Porter was basically the old 'three-threads' but made in one brew. It seems that Harwood's Brewery in Shoreditch was the first to produce this beer, often at first known as 'Entire' — short for 'entire butt beer' — although the 'Porter' name caught on from the 1760s. The companies that went in for large-scale brewing of Porter used enormous vats in its production; one, at the Meux Brewery, had a capacity of 5,760,000 pints and was 30 feet deep and 70 feet in diameter. In 1814, a vat at Meux's Tottenham Court Road brewery burst and a tsunami of porter coursed down the nearby streets. Eight people died and some houses were demolished.

Porter enjoyed around 100 years of prominence on the London brewing and drinking scene after which its popularity declined rapidly, one major reason being that it was thought of first and foremost as a nutritious beer to be quaffed by men who did hard physical labour and by the 1820s mechanisation was taking the place of physical effort in so many productive processes. Porter also suffered from the rise of the lighter-coloured beers, originally from Burton-on-Trent, which gained an ever-increasing share of beer sales. This had a strange side-effect because glass became the most popular material for drinking vessels, people liking to hold their beer up to the light and see what, if anything, was in it that shouldn't be. This couldn't be done with dark porter. With the large-scale adoption of glass, pewter slid out of fashion. The London pewter industry had done very well for a couple of centuries out of the demand for tankards made of that material.

The alehouse almost seamlessly evolved into the public house although the latter has always been an imprecise term. By the eighteenth century, many London alehouses would have had two public rooms: a parlour and the tap room. The tap room might have been the family kitchen where the casks were on stillage, although they may have been kept in a cellar and their contents brought to the customer in a jug. A few alehouses actually had a bar counter by this time. The general tendency was for alehouses to become larger and better appointed, and the role of the alehouse keeper became more complex but also more lucrative. This meant that they often had less need to rely on an additional source of income. A successful publican ideally had to be a man (it was usually a man) of many parts. Today, what he needed would be called managerial and 'interpersonal skills'. He required the physical strength or sufficient strength of personality to keep difficult, possibly violent customers under control, to be polite but discouraging with bores and those who simply wanted to tell him all their problems, to be able to make all his patrons feel welcome and equally important and also to get on with people from right across the social spectrum. He needed patience and a sense of humour. He had to be sure that he didn't drink the profits. He was expected to extend credit to regular customers and he had to be able to handle all the difficult issues that this occupation brought with it. Many alehouse keepers purged their premises of their more criminally-inclined clientele for fear that the brewery to which they were tied might close them down. As many alehouses moved upmarket and became public houses, their clientele became more discriminating and wanted to enjoy their drinks, and so they were happy to see the back of the local ne'er-do-wells.

A pleasant scene in a respectable eighteenth-century establishment.

It helped business to have a toothsome young serving girl on the premises such as the one who Samuel Pepys kissed several times in an alehouse in Blackfriars in 1663 (Pepys could not keep his hands off women). Leering at, making lewd comments to or touching up such serving girls may have been part of the fun but increasingly other facilities for patrons to enjoy were laid on. Cards were available and such things as shove-halfpenny boards, scaled-down billiard tables and even occasionally bowling or skittle alleys. All these, of course, were sprats to catch the mackerel, intended to attract additional custom and to keep it on the premises for longer.

Consumption of beer seems to have risen through the eighteenth century. Estimates suggest that in the 1690s average consumption in England and Wales was two pints of beer a day across the whole population but many adults considerably exceeded that figure. In the 1730s, many ordinary labourers would put away at least four pints a day of strong beer while those whose work was particularly physically demanding might well sink at least a gallon every working day. (They would probably drink more on Sundays). Working men in such hot places as forges and foundries would have beer delivered to them in jugs during the day by regular arrangement with an alehouse nearby. Beer strength increased. The old-fashioned, fairly weak un-hopped ales virtually disappeared and hopped beer was almost universal, most of it stronger than the ales that were replaced. Many beers were flavoured with herbs. Perhaps the most extraordinary-sounding beer was 'cock ale'. This concoction involved steeping dried fruits, spices and a freshly killed cock in a container full of beer.

The influx of beers from provincial brewing centres increased with improvements in road maintenance, the building of canals and river navigations, and further development of coastal shipping. The beer brought to London was mostly bottled, developments in the glass industry having enabled strong green or brown bottles to be manufactured cheaply. A 'consumer consciousness' was developing where the users of alehouses and public houses were becoming more discriminating and they expected a wider range of drinks to be available. Cider grew in popularity. Much of it came from Somerset, Gloucestershire, Herefordshire and Worcestershire, and reached London along the Thames, the upper reaches of which were made navigable in the late seventeenth century. Cider was cheap and could be extremely strong but it never captured a major share of the London drinks market. Alehouses were also selling gin and brandy, although most of these spirits in the eighteenth century were being sold in specialist drinking establishments.

Political sleaze and shady practices in the United Kingdom may have hit the headlines in the last year or two but they are actually nothing new. Before a process of political reform started in the early 1830s, alehouses were used openly as places to treat voters in parliamentary elections. The Whigs and Tories were bitter rivals, and what was more natural than for some alehouses in the London area to become associated with one or other of these parties, and for banquets and booze-ups to be put on in order for politicians to 'persuade' what few voters there were to vote for them.

The general trend of the period up to the 1830s was for alehouses to become more respectable, although there were many that were not, especially those that were unlicensed. However the powers-that-be tended to be more tolerant of alehouses, no longer seeing them in quite the same way as the rallying place for society's ne'er-do-wells and dissident elements. The more disreputable drinking places were now the small dram-shops selling cheap spirits to a distinctly downmarket clientele. These were hovels run by men and women with no pretence other than they were places that provided the means for their customers to gain temporary oblivion. An example was the seedy cellar in St James's run by Tobias Burn, an Irish immigrant, in the 1730s where the customers stood to drink, there being no pretence at home comforts. In 1736, the Middlesex magistrates reckoned that in the area under their jurisdiction, which included much of London north of the river, there were some 3,835 dram-shops. As elsewhere in northern Europe, cheap spirits for a while replaced beer as the favoured tipple but at the same time those who patronised the dram-shops may have abandoned the alehouses because they no longer found the more respectable surroundings so congenial, while the dram-shop remained free from all the licensing controls that surrounded alehouses. Beer had also risen in price, partly because of increasing taxation, and the dram-shop now offered a cheaper option for those whose intention it was to get blind drunk.

A debate that has concentrated the minds of economic and social historians concerns what happened to the standards of living of the British population during the period conveniently, but misleadingly, known as the 'Industrial Revolution', which can loosely be taken as 1750-1830. The issue is a complex one rendering it difficult to generalise because of differences of class, occupation, industry and region or even district. However, speaking in generalisations, we can say that these years were good for the already well-to-do and that many skilled workers maintained the differential of their incomes vis-à-vis the unskilled workers and labourers, the latter being those who were usually the first to be affected by the cyclical fluctuations to which the British economy was increasingly prone. London, with its extremely diverse range of business activity, was less affected than most other places, but it is likely that much of this period was hard for semi-skilled and unskilled workers and their families. It was in these years that the criminal rookeries, such as the 'Holy Land' around Seven Dials and St Giles', were probably at their most menacing. The state of the underworld was always a barometer of the condition of the section of the population next above it in the social hierarchy.

Methodists and other nonconformist sects suffered serious discrimination until the late 1820s, being prevented by law from entering a number of prestigious professions. This meant that the more ambitious of them threw their energy into manufacturing or other kinds of commercial enterprise, and many did this with considerable success, becoming extremely wealthy. The nonconformists had a fervour and apparent conviction about their religious practices that contrasted starkly with the lack of enthusiasm and the moral and spiritual decay of much of the Church of England. The period from the 1770s through to the 1820s saw nonconformists and other largely middle-class evangelical elements attempt a moral regeneration of society. This manifested itself, for example, in the campaign against slavery, an attempt to reinvigorate the Church of England and the establishment of numerous societies for the reformation of manners. This movement was not accidental but was rooted in concerns about growing popular discontent and also the need to inculcate in an unwilling proletariat a disciplined approach to work practices. Industrialists, for example, with tight production schedules to meet could have no truck with casual attitudes that harked back to work on the land where 'St Monday' had often been taken as an unofficial holiday by rural labourers suffering hangovers from excessive drinking on the Sunday. Many of the tasks involved in agricultural work could simply be completed later in the week by working extra hard or putting in longer hours. As industry became more mechanised, such an approach to getting the job done simply could not be tolerated.

Britain's ruling classes had experienced an enormous blow when, largely through their own stupidity, they lost the American colonies. The events in America were followed closely by the French Revolution and Britain's rulers were badly scared by all the evidence of 'people power' and talk of liberty and democracy. Those who thought that they were standing on the moral high ground were actually attempting to maintain social and political stability and to impose the new attitudes required of a pliable industrial workforce.

They were doing this at a time of heightened tensions between the classes. Alehouses and public houses, especially in London but also in a few other big towns, were believed to be the places where dissidents, radicals and revolutionary agitators met to exchange ideas and to plot their evil machinations. The London Corresponding Society chose the Bell in Exeter Street, Covent Garden, for its early meetings. In 1792, the London magistrates simply closed down all the drinking places that hosted meetings of radicals. It was inevitable that measures would be taken to control drinking places, and especially alehouses, more closely. Magistrates actively moved to close down small alehouses, especially those located on the back-alleys and also others about which they had suspicions. They became unwilling to issue new licences, and the result in Southwark, for example, was a decline between 1792 and 1814 of twenty-two licensed premises. Activities that had traditionally taken place in alehouses were curbed. These included the payment of wages in tap rooms, cockfighting, gaming and gambling.

It was not unknown for the organisations concerned to take out prosecutions against individual publicans. In 1802-3, the Society for the Suppression of Vice took over 200 publicans to court for selling drink during the hours of divine service on Sunday mornings. Solicitors working for societies of this kind 'advised' the licensing magistrates by providing evidence of misdoing on the part of publicans. The well-known nineteenth century wit Sydney Smith described these organisations as societies 'for suppressing the vices of persons whose income does not exceed £500 per annum'.

The regulatory attention and supervision that alehouses and public houses received proved too irksome for many publicans who either left the trade or transferred to smaller establishments that were virtually free of control, such as unlicensed alehouses and especially dram-shops. At this time there was far less that the sanctimonious busybodies could do about these places. Although the craze for gin-drinking had died down, there were still many down-at-heel dives selling dubious spirits and their numbers began to grow rapidly once more from the 1780s. Their clientele drew heavily on the unskilled and labouring sections of society who were frequently in and out of work and many were migrants from Ireland and Scotland.

A feature of this period was the increasing domination of London's brewing industry by the large concerns. Truman's brewery increased its annual output from 46,000 barrels in 1750 to 200,800 barrels in 1820, while over the same period Barclay's output rose from 46,100 to 307,200 barrels. There had been 165 brewers in London in 1750 but there were only 56 left in 1823. By 1830, three-quarters of the strong beer consumed in London was produced by just twelve great breweries. These concerns were at the cutting edge in the application of the newest technology and also in a scientific approach to the organisation of their workforces. They increasingly operated houses tied to selling their products either through loans to the publican or leases. By 1800, Barclay Perkins had eighty-eight and Whitbread almost thirty. They were anxious to safeguard the large investments they had made in such places and developed very close relationships with the magistrates. These were on a 'you scratch my back and I'll scratch your back', basis. It was usually possible to come to some sort of arrangement to turn a blind eye when necessary. People wanting to become publicans went to the brewers who could fix it for them with the magistrates. Licensees needed to be mindful of the close relationship between brewers and magistrates if they wanted to stay in the trade. Many of them were thrifty people who had previously been in service — the epitome of respectability. Another occupation that provided recruits for pub keeping was pugilism. Successful prize-fighters were folk-heroes and that could be good for trade. Their skills, of course, might come in handy with fractious customers.

The monopolistic tendencies of the brewing industry in London were not universally welcomed, and in 1805, critics of the big brewers set up the Golden Lane Brewery to try to break their stranglehold. It did not succeed. The publican brewing beer just for sale on his own premises was now virtually extinct. Instead the brewers who dominated the pubs of the metropolis invested in substantial new tailor-made public houses, preferring to run one large house to several smaller ones. These new public houses were generally spacious, well-appointed and designed to be easily supervised from the bar. They were frequently multi-roomed, and the surroundings and the service provided was carefully graded so that men in their working clothes might be welcome in the tap room or the public bar but would not be allowed in the parlour or the lounge if there was one. There might be rooms used for entertainment and also available to be hired for meetings. These public houses had accommodation for the publican and family, and sometimes had guest bedrooms but usually limited provision for the preparation and serving of food. New technology led to the appearance of the now familiar hand-pump on the top of the bar — itself an innovation. The consensus seems to be that the beer engine was invented by the talented engineer Joseph Bramah in 1797. The hand-pump, drawing beer straight from the cask in the cellar, enabled customers to be served very quickly, and the whole purpose of these establishments was a high volume of trade. The name of the establishment was usually now permanent rather than changing with every new publican. Some public houses, perhaps to emphasise the historic provenance and to distinguish themselves from more downmarket watering holes, might call themselves 'tavern' or 'inn'. This served as a source of confusion about the technical or legal distinctions between these places, which has continued to this day.

Beer sales dipped during the period from 1800 to 1830. This was partly because the price of beer was hiked up as fiscal duty was increased. There was a move away to other drinks, not necessarily alcoholic ones, and especially coffee. There was a revival of such spirits as gin and brandy on which the tax actually came down. Also a fall in real wages meant that working people had less disposable income to spend on beer, which was now comparatively expensive. Many cook-shops offered cheaper and more interesting fare than could be found in some alehouses and others also started selling liquor. In addition, a little German chemist by the name of Fredrick Accum published an unexpected best-seller in 1820 with the unremarkable title 'Treatise on Adulterations of Food'. This had a considerable impact because he used his training to blow the whistle on the extremely widespread and unscrupulous practice of adulterating foodstuffs with cheap substitute or additive substances, many of which were harmful to human wellbeing. Everyone knew that brewers and publicans watered their beer to increase their profit margins if they could get away with it, but that paled into insignificance compared to the alarming litany of dubious substances that Accum revealed were added to beer. They included *cocculus indicus*, which is the fruit of an Asian climbing plant and a powerful alkaloid poison related to Deadly Nightshade and also opium.

By the end of the eighteenth century there was pressure for a reform of the licensing laws. Some people believed that the brewing industry, the publicans and their customers would benefit by the removal of all the regulatory measures and

This scene of the late eighteenth century suggests conviviality and general bonhomie.

being subjected to the fresh wind of untrammelled market forces. Others were Liberals who were happy with anything that reduced the power of the big brewers, most of whom were staunch Tories. Others deplored the operation of the large numbers of unlicensed drinking places that worked outside the law but with almost total immunity. They thought that drinking could be cleared up if respectable public houses could be given more freedom for their operations. The force was with the reformers and the result was the Beer Act of 1830. This allowed any 'reputable' householder to sell beer if he had an excise permit and without supervision by the magistrates. The excise duties on beer were repealed. The immediate result was an explosion in the number of drinking places. The beershops sanctioned by this Act were usually small and dingy domestic premises, off the main streets. The customers were almost all taken from the poorer sections of society, and the beershops had all the vices of the most disreputable drinking places of earlier times. Prostitutes hawked their services, drunken fights broke out with some frequency, criminals plotted their activities, stolen property was received and sold, small-time professional gamblers and conmen duped the gullible. Most customers got drunk — a few uproariously so and many severely enough to become ill. Pools of vomit marked their unsteady progress homewards. They were easy game for footpads.

Dickens gives us an idea of what the new beer-houses were like in *Sketches by Boz,* which was illustrated by the zealously anti-drink illustrator Cruikshank. This particular dive was in Scotland Yard, then a very seedy part of Westminster, and it shows a harmless enough scene as several men in their working clothes, clearly coal-heavers by trade, apparently sing away happily with pewter tankards of stout on the table. The room depicted is basic with simple wooden furniture and there is a roaring coal fire. A dog by the fireside adds to the sense of domesticity.

The alehouse had survived so long because it was extremely adaptable and able to perform differing functions at different times, reflecting the changing needs of evolving economic and social circumstances. Governments needed alehouses because they gained so much revenue from the tax on the beer they sold yet they looked askance at them as the place where criminals resorted and, worse than that, dangerous men concocted vile political plots. They were, however, integral to the life of the plebeian communities they served and in them their mostly male customers gained at least some relief from their brutish existence. An observer in the 1720s summed up the ambivalent nature of these places:

> The vile obscene talk, noise, nonsense and ribaldry discourses together with the fumes of tobacco, belchings and other foul breakings of wind, that are generally found in an ale-room...are enough to make any rational creature among them almost ashamed of his being. But all this, the rude rabble esteem the highest degree of happiness and run themselves into the greatest straits imaginable to attain it.

Chapter 7

The Rise of the Gin-Palaces and the Emergence of the Victorian Pub

Gin was like a gadfly. It was a persistent malign feature of London life through much of the eighteenth and the nineteenth centuries. George Cruikshank, the cartoonist, was a leading campaigner against the evils associated with drink and in 1833 he commented, 'Gin has become a great demi-god, a mighty spirit dwelling in gaudy, gold-beplastered temples.' The middle classes were deeply concerned that gin was causing the lower classes to self-destruct. Crime, they said, was out of control, and gin was the cause. A few years earlier an earnest would-be reformer had stood outside a gin shop in Holborn where, to his amazed horror, he saw no fewer than six people entering the premises every minute. Doing a quick calculation, he made that a total of 360 people going into the place in just 1 hour. Curiously, he does not mention how many left in that time but presumably there were some who came out otherwise it would have become uncomfortably crowded. The place on whose comings and goings he was spying was the well-known Thompson and Fearon's on Holborn Hill, demolished to make way for the construction of Holborn Viaduct, which was completed in 1869.

The Beer Act of 1830 had been an attempt to counter the insidious influence of gin by making beer far cheaper and more readily available. While it led to a rapid proliferation in the number of establishments selling beer, places selling gin continued to prosper and indeed to increase in numbers. By the middle of the 1830s, the term 'gin palace' had become established, although it was always imprecise. Gin palaces were places that sought to hide the essentially sleazy nature of their trade by surrounding the drinker with florid and resplendent furniture and fittings. These included painted murals, decorative and sometimes pictorial tiling inside and out, polished brass work, large mirrors, much bright gas-lighting, a mass of polished mahogany woodwork, etched glass windows and elaborate plasterwork. These gorgeous surroundings flattered their largely working class clientele in the same way that the plush cinemas of the 1920s and 1930s gave their patrons a temporary sense of being cocooned in luxury. Both the nineteenth- and the twentieth-century customers were escaping from lives that were, otherwise, at best drab. The brewers who invested large amounts of money in these drinking places did so because they had serendipitously realised that although individually impoverished drinkers had little money, if they could be attracted to these outlets *en masse* then they had considerable spending power.

By no means all the establishments selling gin were furnished in this way. Many of them were smaller and far more simply furnished, and most of them sold beer as well as gin and other spirits. They also sold drink to be taken away and consumed off the premises. The bad name that these places had was at least partly the result of middle-class hysteria and the propaganda of the anti-drink lobby. It may also be because the introduction in London of modern policing from around 1830 led to the reporting and prosecution of far more drink-related crime. The gin palaces in their opulence contrasted starkly with the vast majority of London's existing drinking places which were small and humble enough as to be virtually indistinguishable from the workaday housing with which they were surrounded. Many of these establishments were simply domestic premises having a small public part given over to selling drink and unlikely even to have a bar counter.

Dickens in *Sketches by Boz* describes one of the new gin palaces located in a dingy working class area:

> ...the gay building with the fantastically ornamented parapet, the illuminated clock, the plate-glass windows surrounded by stucco rosettes, and its profusion of gas-lights in richly-gilt burners, is perfectly dazzling when contrasted with the dirt and darkness we have just left. The interior is even gayer than the exterior. A bar of French-polished mahogany, elegantly carved, extends the whole width of the place...

The temperance people certainly did not like London's basic drinking establishments but they absolutely loathed the gin palaces, seeing them as brazenly flaunting the insidious evil they believed was undermining the mores of contemporary society. Many gin palaces were indeed located close to notorious slum districts whose half-starved inhabitants with their empty bellies obviously became drunk very quickly when they downed cheap gin. The squalid and unsavoury results could be seen on the streets of London day in and day out. The temperance activists blamed the brewers, the publicans and the impoverished slum-dwellers who could just manage to afford a quick fix. They never turned their anger on an economic system which created vast wealth but allocated resources in such a way that large parts of the population were condemned to work for poverty wages and to live in housing unfit for human habitation.

The technological advances associated with the Industrial Revolution had huge significance for the brewing industry. From the late eighteenth century, steam power was being harnessed for many parts of the brewing process and this involved a level of capital investment usually beyond the range of smaller brewers. The use of steam in breweries enabled the mass production of beer. Gas-lighting made its initial appearance on London's streets around 1809. Increasingly through the nineteenth century it was being used to good effect

A typically imposing street corner pub in the City. Eldon Street, EC2.

for eye-catching lamps outside pubs and also to illuminate their interiors, particularly after the incandescent gas mantle was invented in 1885. Bright lights both outside and inside pubs must have contrasted with the stygian interiors of many of the customers' own dwellings and the surrounding streets, especially in the earlier part of the century. Technical progress elsewhere enabled large sheets of glass to be made much more cheaply and lavish use was made of glass for the windows, interior divisions of the pubs and for mirrors, which, of course, reflected light and increased the sense of space. The ending of the tax on glass in the mid-nineteenth century was a great help. It was the gin palaces that made the most sumptuous use of gas and glass but few London pubs, even down at the humbler end of things, were unaffected, although on a smaller scale. Another technological innovation, the beer engine, with its characteristic handle atop the bar, has been mentioned previously and became almost universal in London's pubs, enabling ales and beers to be drawn from the cask and dispensed very quickly.

London's population rose from less than a million in 1801 to over two million in 1841. This opened up great opportunities for the licensed trade. Brewers and publicans were motivated by the need not only to keep the customers coming in but to try to win new clients and to get them all to stay longer and spend more money. They saw the need to diversify the services that were offered. Public taste is capricious and it was important to keep one jump ahead. An extreme example of entrepreneurial enterprise was the *Eagle Tavern* in City Road. This was the establishment that was immortalised in the ditty:

Up and down the City Road,
In and out the *Eagle,*
That's the way the money goes,
Pop goes the weasel.

Hidden in this verse is the pub's connection with the leather trade, in particular with saddlers. They used a tool called a 'weasel' for punching holes in the leather they were working on. Some of the less thrifty workers in the trade found themselves short of beer money before pay day and so they 'popped' their weasels as a pledge with the landlord who acted as a pawnbroker.

The *Eagle* had been a small and fairly unremarkable tavern for some years although unusual for having a tea garden at the rear. It was acquired by Thomas Rouse in the 1820s and under his stewardship it enjoyed many years as one of the most popular of London's pleasure resorts. The grounds were turned into to a pleasure garden with statues, fountains, illuminations, an orchestra, refreshments and a variety of live entertainments. The piece de resistance was probably the Grecian Saloon. This had started in a humble way as a place for small-scale entertainment in an upper room of the original tavern. Its popularity was such that in 1831 Rouse erected a purpose-built 'Saloon' in the garden which was larger than the tavern! This looked rather silly and so Rouse next had the tavern itself rebuilt in 1839-40. It was an enormous and imposing classical building which towered above the neighbourhood.

Rouse, who was a builder, was clearly not the understated sort because the building was surmounted by four carved eagles looking superciliously down on the surrounding district, each being perched on a tablet which bore Rouse's name. It was luxuriously appointed inside and had a ballroom which doubled as a concert room large enough to accommodate several hundred people. The *Eagle* was a grand place and catered for well-to-do clientele. Some experts take the *Eagle* as the origin of the music hall.

We have said that fashion is capricious but the *Eagle* had a long run at the head of its field. Dickens knew it well and in *Sketches by Boz* his characters Jemima Evans and Samuel Wilkins pay it a visit. The pub and its music hall were still going in the 1870s and the immortal Marie Lloyd, she who was described as the possessor of the most suggestive wink in show business, performed there at the age of 14. Ironically the building was sold to the Salvation Army in 1884 and demolished in 1901. A replacement *Eagle Tavern* was built close by at the junction with Shepherdess Walk, N1 and is still trading.

As London spread outwards, the fields and trees disappeared under bricks and mortar, the big landowners parcelling out their land for development and speculative builders erecting a whole block of streets or sometimes just a row or two of residential properties. In the more densely-populated working class areas, pubs were erected almost on every street corner, in the confident belief that they would be eagerly snapped up by individuals or the big brewers, looking for a potentially lucrative business. These were often small and simple establishments. In the areas designed for middle-class occupation, there were fewer houses per square mile and fewer pubs although sometimes those that were provided were massive and frequently had some eye-catching feature such as a dome or tower with a clock in it. Wherever possible, these pubs, both small and large, were built on corners so that in theory they could pick up trade from the intersection of two or more streets. Sometimes the pub was the first building to be completed and the builder himself might be the initial licensee. He would use the pub as his site office and a base for his workers and then sell the lease to the pub once there were enough houses nearby to provide a potential clientele. A theoretical working ratio was one pub to 160 dwellings. In the areas containing the most prestigious and expensive housing, the only pubs might be those hidden away in the mews and used by domestic servants and to a lesser extent by residents. Belgravia provided examples of this practice.

The disposition, relative size and the function of the various rooms in these purpose-built pubs varied enormously depending on the district and the kind of clientele that was expected. The bar as the main place for service was now a dominant feature and there might be any variation on rooms with names such as tap room, public bar, bar parlour, parlour and possibly private bar, saloon, coffee room, club room, news room, commercial room and, very occasionally, smoke room. Some of these rooms would have table service and were equipped with bells to attract the attention of the waiting staff. The more basic rooms downstairs would have little or no seating. Many pubs had rooms for hire upstairs and the largest of these might metamorphose into a concert room. If entertainment in such a room proved to be successful, an extension might be made to the pub to house what in effect was a music hall. The larger establishments might have a kitchen where food was prepared for consumption in a dining room or in a 'song and supper room' or saloon where customers could be entertained as they dined. This practice met with the disapproval of the authorities who in 1843 decreed that they either registered as theatres, thereby losing the right to serve drinks where the entertainment took place, or they ceased to put on any entertainment that could loosely be described as 'theatrical'. Some of these then went off and either became music halls or theatres pure and simple. The music hall as an entertainment venue is inextricably linked with London in the nineteenth century.

Links developed between pubs, music halls and theatres. It was not always easy to classify individual examples. An example of a hybrid creation was Evans's Song and Supper Room in Covent Garden. This was more than a 'room'. It was a large and magnificent hall opened in 1855 on the site of a popular but much smaller establishment known for its bawdy and boisterous entertainment. The customers were provided with excellent fare and they ate or drank, smoked and conversed while musical and other entertainments of a somewhat more refined nature took place. Ladies were not allowed in the auditorium. This place was certainly not a pub although it provided beer, wine and spirits. Nor was it a music hall, the prime purpose of which was entertainment. By no manner of means could it be described as a theatre. Such illustrations as exist of this and similar establishments like the Oxford Music Hall in Oxford Street show the patrons seemingly oblivious to their splendid surroundings and equally oblivious to the performances taking place on the stage. They do, however, appear to be behaving decorously. The differences between pubs, pleasure gardens, theatres, music halls, song and supper rooms, etc., were never clearly defined.

One location which drew the opprobrium of the writer of an article in the 'London City Mission Magazine' in 1870 was Battersea Fields, then a fairly rustic location but close enough to attract large numbers of Londoners especially on warm weekends. He directed his disapproval at the Red House and Balloon pubs and the Sunday fairs held close by. He said:

> ...if ever there was a place out of hell that surpassed Sodom and Gomorrah in ungodliness and abomination, this was it. Here the worst men and vilest of the human race seemed to try to outvie each other in wicked deeds. I have gone to this sad spot on the afternoon and evening of the Lord's day, where there have been from 60 to 120 horses and donkeys racing, foot-racing, walking matches, flying boats, flying horses, roundabouts, theatres, comic actors, shameless dancers, conjurors, fortune-tellers, gamblers of every description, drinking-booths, stalls, hawkers and vendors of all kinds of articles. It would take a more graphic pen than mine to describe the mingled shouts and noises and the unmentionable doings of this pandemonium on earth.

The Victorian middle-class looked loftily down on the 'unwashed masses'. They saw them as a pool of potential criminality and as boorish, brutish and insufficiently servile. Too many of them seemed dangerously irreligious and ungrateful for the role in life which the Almighty had in his wisdom decreed for them. Some of the institutions of self-help that were created such as technical institutions, mechanics' institutes and public libraries were often the result of well-meaning philanthropy but they nevertheless smacked to some extent of condescension and were easily seen as being patronising. They certainly provided one route among various others that were taken by some working men (but not many women) to climb out of poverty and ascend the social ladder. They had little relevance, however, for the bulk of working men for whom the pub in Victorian England played a central role. The pub was 'their' haven, their institution. It was where they could unwind and relax with their friends and other members of their class and in that sense, the London pub of the nineteenth century was very much a working-class institution deeply embedded in the popular culture of the time.

The St Giles and Seven Dials area, ironically known as the 'Holyland', largely cleared when New Oxford Street, Charing Cross Road and Shaftesbury Avenue were built in the 1880s, was one of London's most notorious and dangerous criminal rookeries, penetrated by strangers at their peril. In 1844 a journalist had visited a beerhouse called 'Rat Castle' where he found 'low ceilinged, wretched rooms filled with desperadoes and youthful thieves'. He went on to say that the human occupants were more brutalised than the bulldogs and specialised rat-catching curs who circulated freely and were perfectly at home in this hovel. However, the fact was that the vast majority of those who used London's pubs were not engaged in plotting criminal activity or political subversion, were not fighting drunk, not going home to beat up their wives and were not spending the bulk of their frugal weekly income on booze at the expense of the family. This was something that those who wished to mould the morals of the working class were simply too blind to see. The workers' own self-help organisations, the trade unions and the friendly societies very often had their meetings in pubs. Many of their members were serious-minded, determined to rise themselves and wanting to raise the class to which they belonged and they thought that the influence of alcohol was deleterious to those processes. However, the pub was the natural space for them to carry out their collective activities. The anti-drink lobby did not like that either, of course.

In working-class residential districts, the significance of the pub in the life of the community must be seen in the context of the fact that the street and especially the street corner were the places that acted as the focus of the social life of all ages. The street, unless it was a very busy highway, united rather than divided the community. The pavements were alive with human activity. Shops were more like stalls, being less cut off from the streets than were the shops which replaced them. Many people made their living out on the street — stallholders, entertainers, pedlars, hucksters, organ-grinders, beggars, con-men and pickpockets. Potmen from the pub hurried to and fro carrying cans of ale to regular customers in nearby workplaces. Children sent to the pub with a jug, surreptitiously took a sip or two of beer on the way home. Life was lived on the street -it was a very public forum. The pub was an extension of it but it offered that little bit of privacy behind frosted glass for those recreational and even business activities where some privacy was desirable but the comfort, the warmth, the bright lights and the convivial buzz were something that only the communality of the pub could offer. Incidentally an act in 1901 prohibited the sale of intoxicants unless they were in corked, sealed containers, to children under fourteen.

An everyday scene in a down-to-earth working-class pub.

Dickens crossed swords with the anti-drink lobby. He was well aware of alcohol abuse and the problems to which it led. However, in a review of an allegorical story full of the woes brought on by drink called *The Drunkard's Children,* he says:

> Drunkenness, as a national horror, is the effect of many causes. Foul smells, disgusting habitations, bad workshops and workshop customs, want of light, air and water, the absence of all easy means of decency and health, are commonest among its common, everyday physical causes...

From the mid-1840s, Britain entered a period of about fifty or more years, characterised, despite periodic blips, by economic growth and rising real incomes and living standards. From about 1850 to 1880, Britain's position as the 'Workshop of the World' was virtually unchallenged. London's pubs reflected these developments. Large numbers of middle class and working class people had more disposable income than ever before and consumption of spirits and beer rose to peaks in, respectively, 1875 and 1876. Many of the capital's pubs were rebuilt and new ones were opened on a grandiose scale, even if their architectural style could, at best, be described as 'eclectic'. The furniture and fittings of the best of them were absolutely of the highest quality. The speculator who built pubs could make a fortune. Dickens did not like the brash new establishments. He deplored the knocking down of the old familiar drinking houses and the depositing as he put it of 'splendid mansions, stone balustrades, rosewood fittings, immense lamps, and illuminated clocks, at the corner of every street'.

As the consumption of alcohol increased, so the hostility of its critics grew more strident. Sunday, supposedly the day for public worship and the pursuit of peaceful contemplation, was the day of the week when fewest people were at work and a time given over by many working class Londoners to serious drinking — what would now be described as 'binge-drinking'. As the law stood in the early 1820s, pubs were not allowed to sell drinks during the hours of divine service. Although the nineteenth century was by no means the period of intense religious observation that it is sometimes portrayed as having been, there were many who felt that they still ought to attend worship. They often did this after a drinking bout and the consequence was that many church services were interrupted by fighting and other loutish behaviour. Worshippers who had been in the pub previously might suddenly rush out of church to attend to the calls of nature and it was not unknown for others to throw up violently. With this kind of thing happening, those imbibers who merely came to church and then promptly fell asleep, snoring in the pews, were almost welcomed. In 1839 London's pubs were required to close between midnight on Saturday and noon on Sunday. This measure was resented by dyed-in-the-wool drinkers who saw it as a waste of half a Sunday.

In pre-industrial and urban England, there had been a natural symbiosis of church and pub. Both had been at the heart of the community. The pub was often close to the churchyard. The various parochial meetings took place in the pub and the priest presided over the church-ales. Worshippers and bell-ringers slaked their thirsts in the pub after and sometimes before the service. It was a mark of changed economic and social realities that the two institutions of church and pub

A Phil May cartoon from 1894. It is titled 'Q.E.D.' and the caption went: "What's up wi' Sal?"
"Ain't yer 'erd? She's married agin!" Drink and domestic violence were two sides of the same coin.

were now rivals, both trying to canvass for the minds, the bodies and the money of the urban masses.

Whereas early temperance activists had merely condemned spirits, by the 1850s many of them were campaigning for the total prohibition of alcohol production and retailing. Even among those who opposed this idea, a received wisdom developed that a drastic reduction in the number of places selling alcohol was needed. The pro-drink lobby responded and acts of parliament were passed in 1869 and 1872 representing a considerable emasculation of what the temperance, teetotal and prohibitionist supporters had wanted. They had to make do for the time being with a reduction in opening hours and more stringent fines for drunkenness and infringement of the licensing laws. The beer-houses now came under the control of the licensing magistrates. The number of licensed premises now began to fall but at first only usually because of repeated infringements of the law by licensees or agreements with the brewers that they would issue a license for a new pub on condition that the brewery concerned surrendered the licenses of two or more of their existing houses. There were magistrates who were bitterly hostile to the licensed trade but rarely, in London at least, in a majority at any one time and they usually had to be content to go along with the consensus among their colleagues that a reduction in the number of pubs was desirable. The smaller pubs were often the victims of this conviction, the magistrates preferring larger, new pubs designed in such a way as to make supervision by the staff easier.

Chapter 8

The Victorian Public House
Comes of Age

London continued to expand at a phenomenal rate. The slow but steady and seemingly inexorable decline in the number of beer-houses and pubs meant that by 1900 there were significantly fewer drinking places per head of the population. With new licenses being difficult to obtain, some districts contained very few pubs. Sometimes those individuals or organisations that owned the land on which new housing development took place refused to allow any pubs at all, the Artisans, Labourers & General Dwellings Company being an example on large-scale schemes it carried out at Noel Park, Hornsey and Queen's Park. London's outward spread absorbed large numbers of what had previously been peripheral villages. Some had highly rustic pubs, which, quickly overwhelmed by increasing demand, were rebuilt, enlarged and updated.

In spite of the generally hostile attitude of the magistrates to the licensed trade, some mainly working class districts contained what to us today seem to be very large numbers of pubs. An example is Camberwell which, as late as the 1820s, was a village set among fields and woods where the eponymous Camberwell Beauty butterfly could be found. Urban development began in earnest about 1830 and by 1837 there were 138 pubs and 96 beer-shops. In 1902 Camberwell was a densely populated suburban district home to a largely working class and lower middle class population. In that year it had 302 premises licensed for on-sales plus 130 off-licenses. This worked out at around one pub for every 800 residents.

Ironically, the fact that the number of drinking houses generally failed to keep pace with the increasing population was an advantage for some publicans who found themselves in the happy situation of significantly increased demand. They themselves, or the brewers where tied houses were involved, met this demand by altering their premises so that they could supply larger numbers of customers more quickly and efficiently. One means of doing so was to redesign the interior to make more effective use of the space. The introduction of the u-shaped or promontory bar

This is a surprising survivor of a small back street local boozer. Pear Tree Court, E2.

from the 1870s and later the island bar greatly increased the length of the counter at which customers could be served. Most custom-built pubs had a 'jug-and-bottle' department for off-sales. Large numbers of glittering mirrors not only acted as advertisements and added to the sense of light and space, they also enabled staff to keep a discreet eye on what the customers were doing in the pub's inner nooks and crannies.

The fashion in the nineteenth century and right through to 1914, unlike today, was for the interior particularly of larger pubs to contain a number of small rooms, each catering for slightly different requirements on the part of their users. Particularly in the more affluent residential areas, the male members of well-to-do families and their male domestic servants might well use the same pub but neither group had any wish to socialise with each other while doing so. Therefore they would inhabit different parts of the pub and the better-off customers might be allowed some privacy by the use of 'snob-screens'. These were ingenious hinged panels of frosted glass placed in a row on the top of the bar at head height and they could be opened if the customer wanted to communicate with the bar staff or see what was going on elsewhere in the pub. They were once very common in London but few have survived. The Lamb in Lamb's Conduit Street, WC1 is one pub which still features this attractive fitting. Big pubs were very much designed with social class in mind and some even had two public bars one reserved for 'superior' working men such as artisans and the other given over to 'common labourers'.

In the latter part of the nineteenth century the word 'saloon' starts coming into use referring to a largish, comfortably-furnished room in the pub which had perhaps been fashioned out of some existing smaller spaces or, in the case of a brand new pub, had been designed as an integral part of it. Saloons were to be found in many of the large establishments and some of the biggest also had a large room with several tables where billiards could be played. It might be called a 'billiard saloon' and it clearly was designed to attract customers and keep them on the premises, slaking their thirsts frequently while engaged in play. Inter-pub billiards competitions could also attract a lot of hard-drinking custom.

The enemies of alcohol never rested. The more perceptive of them realised that working people, especially men, did not frequent pubs simply to get drunk. Even they had to admit that most of the habitués rarely, if ever, became more than mildly intoxicated. The pub clearly served other purposes for its working class clientele, not least the opportunity to socialise in cheerful surroundings. We should not be surprised to learn that the temperance people set up coffee public houses which had all the facilities of pubs except for the alcoholic drinks. They did, however, provide food of a standard superior to the vast majority of pubs. The first of these establishments opened in Dundee in 1853 and the concept reached London in 1872 when the philanthropist Dr Barnardo bought a notorious pub in Limehouse in the East End and reopened it after refurbishment as the Edinburgh Castle Coffee Palace. The idea caught on to the extent that by 1884 there were 121 similar establishments in the capital. They sold other beverages than simply coffee, provided games such as billiards, encouraged their patrons to attend lectures on 'improving' subjects and organised excursions — all without recourse to the 'Demon Drink'. There were even drinks available that looked and tasted rather like beer. A notable example was

'Cox's Anti-Burton', a bottled imitation of mild ale. The labels proudly informed the reader that this concoction had been awarded first prize by the Ely Diocesan branch of the Church of England Temperance Society — an accolade if ever there was one.

Nineteenth century temperance activists had their roots with the puritans of the sixteenth and seventeenth centuries but they began to gain influence in the north of England in the 1830s. Theobald Matthew was one of the most zealous temperance missionaries and he would address large outdoor meetings abjuring them to moderate their use of alcohol and to make a public declaration by 'taking the pledge'. He was enough of an attraction to be mobbed by a largely friendly crowd of 20,000 when he spoke at Blackheath on the occasion of his first visit to London. More extreme was the teetotal movement whose leader for a period in the 1830s was Joseph Livesey. Moderation was not enough for them — they wanted total abstinence. The judgemental and sanctimonious nature of much of the temperance and abolitionist propaganda, rubbed the people for whom it was intended, up the wrong way. Material with biblical quotes, usually from the Old Testament , was lost on people who were staunchly irreligious. Poor people were not poor simply because they drank. Why, they asked, was so little said about the private drinking of the middle and upper-classes? After all, the expression was 'as drunk as a lord', not 'as drunk as a dustman'.

By the 1880s brewing, pubs and beer consumption had arrived on the party political agenda. The Conservatives were generally seen as supporters of the brewing industry and the Liberals as its increasingly bitter opponent. There was a strong nonconformist and prohibition group within the Liberals but their ability to mount the kind of effective action they would have liked was prevented by the extreme factionalism within the party and the fact that they spent much time out of office until enjoying a landslide victory in 1906. Under the Tories, beer sales went up, more people including women, were drinking and there was a boom in the enlarging, remodelling and general enhancement of many of London's pubs.

The brewers directly owned a smaller proportion of pubs in London than elsewhere. In 1892 they owned less than a third, partly because the price of land was so high in the Metropolis. By that time, however, some of the major brewers from Burton-on-Trent, the largest English brewing centre outside London, were aggressively addressing the London market, buying up existing pubs and opening new ones and supplying them with their own products. These were light pale ales and bitters, very different from the familiar London porters, containing as they did traces of gypsum from the aquifers under Burton. The Midland Railway Company developed a very lucrative traffic moving beer, much of it in special fast freight trains from Burton to Somers Town Goods Depot whence much of it was briefly stored securely in the huge undercroft beneath St Pancras station before being distributed around the capital. The breweries involved included Worthington and Bass, Ratcliff and Gretton.

The London brewers reacted to what they saw as a very serious threat by themselves acquiring large numbers of pubs and rebuilding and extending their existing estates, raising the money to do so by a public flotation of shares. A business war broke out in the race to buy up outlets and among those taking part quarter was neither given nor expected. The price of pubs went through the roof. Pub architects were on a roll. Even publicans got in on the act and bought a house or two. A few built up small portfolios of pubs. However, it was a financial bubble based on borrowed money and, as is the nature of such things, it eventually burst. The year was 1899.

So the period from the mid-1880s to the first decade of the twentieth century was one which saw many new pubs built and existing ones frequently changing hands and being enlarged. Brewers wanted large houses with high turnovers — big was beautiful. Some of London's externally most ostentatious pubs date from this period and the internal fittings were often of exceptional quality and the attention to detail second to none. The fine art world has always been sniffy about 'popular art'. It would be too easy to belittle these pubs for being architecturally eclectic, tasteless, brash and vulgar and perhaps they are but they were products of their time, a fleeting historical moment and in their size and florid external appearance, they were making a statement. In effect it was a two-fingered gesture to censorious middle class opinion. A few examples were the Queen's, Crouch End N8, the Elgin, Ladbroke Grove W10, the Warrington, Warrington Crescent W9 and the Salisbury, Green Lanes, N4. A small example was, and is, the famed Red Lion, Duke of York Street SW1, fairly unremarkable on the outside but with a riot of sparkling mirrors and etched glass inside.

Such buildings spared little expense in ensuring that they were eye-catching and dominated their surroundings and that they would entice the drinker in and then keep him or more rarely her, sometimes both, there. The decorative brickwork, ornamental plastering and bright lamps hanging from wrought iron brackets outside caught the eye, the bright lights inside and the rich decorative window glass suggested a welcoming and luxurious interior. Even the lobbies were often mini art galleries on their walls containing fine tiled pictures. Inside was an extravaganza of glittering mirrors, etched and enamelled and sometimes embossed or etched opaque glass and decorative plasterwork, often made with proprietary imitation materials such as Lyncrusta, composed of canvas and pulped linseed and Anaglypta which was not unlike papier-mâché. Additionally, elaborate polished woodwork of teak, walnut and mahogany and sometimes marblework, provided the sense of a luxurious and warm welcome. The customer entering for the first time would quickly be aware that the interior was made up of a number of smallish compartments, often with low wood and glass screens dividing them from their neighbours as well as perhaps a number of larger rooms. These gave him the choice of a quiet, semi-private drink or a larger, more public space where he might find convivial company if he wished it. Lower middle class and working class customers felt flattered by being able to relax in such opulent surroundings, which would have contrasted starkly with the drabness of most of their homes and workplaces. This was their night out. No effort was spared to get them in the door and once they were there, to encourage them to stay and to spend. It was widely believed that the selling of food gave an establishment a sense of respectability and might attract wider custom. There were even primitive ancestors of jukeboxes in the form of musical automata for the delectation of those who liked a little musical entertainment.

In 1902 the Licensing Act was passed. The licensed trade was in difficulties and this act, by giving stronger powers to the magistrates, generally pleased the anti-drink lobby. In parts of London it became increasingly difficult to extend or upgrade pubs let alone to build new ones. The result is that many pubs became rather rundown in the years up to 1914 and this only tended to worsen the bad name that the drinks trade had in some quarters. With relatively few new pubs being built and not many redesigns and refurbishments, it is hard to pinpoint a characteristic pub style of the period from 1900 to 1914. There was, however, definitely a harking back to some imaginary 'Merrie England'. The result was the appearance of small numbers of pubs masquerading very loosely as 'taverns'. This was essentially a gimmick as the pubs concerned bore little resemblance to the taverns of old London and more to some kind of pastiche of how the country inns of Shakespeare's day were supposed to have looked. In fact, this was perhaps the beginning of the 'Brewer's Tudor' concept which was such a feature of new and rebuilt pubs in the 1920s and 1930s. Non-structural half-timbering, exposed interior brickwork, bottle glass and fake internal timber beams were typical motifs. A few such pubs were located round Fleet Street and the Strand, for example, and more in the outer suburbs. William Younger's Brewery of Edinburgh was particularly keen on half-timbering on some of its London houses.

Before 1900 some kind of pattern was emerging so far as the location and distribution of pubs was concerned. The areas around the big wholesale markets were well supplied with pubs as were the areas around the docks. Many of the major roads out of London had an enormous number of drinking places. At the turn of the twentieth century one stretch of Whitechapel Road boasted a total of forty-eight pubs in just one mile. Such an artery saw an intensive service of trams and pubs tended to follow such lines of communication and fronted streets of densely-packed working class housing as well as a wide range of industrial premises. Residents of the East End who were employed in central London would stop off on their way to work for breakfast and a beer. They might well pop in on the way home as well. Major road junctions might sport a large number of pubs. There were six at Elephant and Castle, five at Cambridge Circus and four at St George's Circus. Conversely, as the importance of the Thames as a means of moving about London declined, so the number of riverside pubs fell significantly.

In areas of London where the rich lived, the population density was far less but there could still be a large number of pubs because the rich had vast armies of servants, living on the premises or travelling to and fro daily. Thus snooty St James's in 1896 had one pub for every 116 inhabitants whereas Edmonton in north-east London which was primarily a working-class suburb only had one pub for every 727 residents. Where one, often aristocratic, landowner dominated a district, there might be a determination to maintain the perceived quality of the area by discouraging the riff-raff and allowing few or sometimes, any, pubs. Pimlico and Bloomsbury were examples. Ironically, this might mean that the districts on the perimeter of such estates might have large numbers of pubs for the refreshment of the domestic staff in the big houses. Some landowners who had no objection to pubs per se, nevertheless wanted them to be as unobtrusive as possible on their estates and they had them tucked away largely out of sight in the mews. Belgravia has several such pubs — small and discreet. The affluent quarters tended to abound in off-licenses where the well-to-do stocked up on their wines and spirits which they consumed in the privacy of their own homes. Another factor influencing the location and density of pubs was the major London railway termini. None of these, of course, could really be said to be in central London with the possible exceptions of Charing Cross and Victoria. However these stations became major transport hubs. As such they attracted huge numbers of users and various facilities were provided for these people close to the stations themselves. The railway termini tended not to be located in London's most fashionable areas and indeed to this day, the surroundings of many them can fairly be described as 'seedy'. Large numbers of pubs in the side streets are still a feature of the districts around Victoria, Paddington and Kings Cross, for example.

Mention has been made of coffee-houses which had exhibitions of curios and this tradition was carried on in the late nineteenth century by a number of pubs which had collections of material which acted as a gimmick to help to bring new customers in. The Mackerel in the Mile End Road, Whitechapel somehow managed to squeeze in no fewer than 20,000 stuffed animals in glass display cases. The World's End in Camden drew thirsty entomologists from afar because it had large numbers of preserved exotic butterflies and ferocious-looking beetles on display. The Edinburgh Castle at Mornington Crescent got the punters through the doors with the aid of a collection of bric-a-brac of dubious provenance including a stuffed pig which appeared to have two bodies and the spear which had supposedly administered the coup de grace on General Gordon at Khartoum. If these and various other

The Monster, a curiously-named pub which, with its associated tea garden, was in Pimlico.

antediluvian artefacts failed to hold the attention, there was a clutch of great auk eggs to fall back on, although not literally.

With so many relatively well-paid men working in central London, especially in the City, there was a huge demand for eating places providing food especially around mid-day. Various kinds of establishments appeared to cater for this demand, which sold beer as an accompaniment to food but were not exactly pubs. Close to Billingsgate, for example, there was a fish restaurant with an excellent reputation where a fine seafood meal could be had for about 1s 6d with various ales and beers to accompany it. Some pubs branched out to provide dining rooms or even a restaurant alongside their more normal drinking spaces. Some of the more old-fashioned taverns and chop-houses acted as reminders of the past. An example was the *Cock* in Fleet Street known for the quality of its chops and steaks. It refused to admit female diners. An advert for the Daniel Lambert Hotel & Tavern in Ludgate Hill shows what is quite clearly a rather up-market bar described as a 'saloon bar' and a 'grill room' where diners can select their chop or steak and watch it being cooked, if they choose to. The Horse Shoe, Tottenham Court Road was an absolutely enormous establishment opened around 1875, which on its ground floor originally had a grill room, a luncheon bar, a large café and an estaminet which was a forerunner of the bistro. Not content with these, there were large dining rooms on the first floor. Such an establishment represented an enormous investment by its owners, the Meux Brewery.

Chapter 9

The Pub Signs of London

As is only to be expected of such a historic, diverse and cosmopolitan city as London, its pub names and signs are a rich source of insights into various aspects of the capital's fascinating and often quirky past. The pub signs of Britain have been described as 'A great open-air portrait gallery' and nowhere does the gallery contain as many interesting signs as London. In 1393 Richard II made it a legal requirement for a drinking place to display a sign so that the ale-taster, whose congenial job would now be described as quality assurance, would know where all the pubs were so that he could check them out. Here we provide a few samples of this diversity, roughly grouped together by theme.

Sign boards and trade signs owe their origins to the need for traders to advertise their businesses at a time when the vast majority of the population was illiterate. Something eye-catching was needed that would provide an immediate indication as to the business being carried on at the premises. Back in Roman times, taverns often advertised their presence with a bunch of greenery, a grapevine or even some actual grapes and these symbolised the fact that wine was available. Today's pubs with names like the Bunch of Grapes or the Grapevine are often reminders of this. Other trade signs are rare these days. Still relatively familiar are the three brass balls of the pawnbroker or the white and red pole of what are now hairdressers but used to be barber-surgeons. Occasionally chemists display a pestle and mortar as reminders of their origins as apothecaries. A pair of shears may indicate a tailor's premises and occasionally other signs can be seen. An ancient and almost forgotten type of sign indicating drinks for sale was a chequerboard frieze around windows or doors. This was a reference to board games being available inside for those who wanted a game with their drinks. One of the last pubs to maintain this practice was the City of Salisbury in Tooley Street, SE1. Ironically, this pub was only built around 1888 and the use of such a device was distinctly anachronistic especially on a modern purpose-built pub. Mind you, the City of Salisbury also had a parapet aping the machicolation of many medieval castles — a projection from the top of the wall allowing defenders to drop missiles on attackers directly below.

Pub names recorded as early as the fourteenth century include a cluster with such names as the Maiden, the Cock, and the Bell, all of these being suffixed by 'On the Hoop' and one still trading, the Hoop and Grapes in Aldgate High Street, EC3. This 'hoop' element in pub names has almost entirely died out. Its meaning is disputed. Some people argue that it refers to the staves or hoops around a barrel end. Others think that it recalls the practice of displaying the greenery or vine wound around a metal hoop. Painted sign boards advertising a tavern or alehouse probably date back to about the same time. They sometimes hung from a bracket on the front of the building or they were atop a free-standing pole close to the building. These two variations are of course familiar today. Another type of sign was a carving, sometimes in the form of a relief or even a three-dimensional representation of a bull for example. Many signs, however, were simple, cheap boards and it was not uncommon for a publican to bring the sign from his previous house and re-erect it when he took over a new one. Likewise if he moved on, he took the sign with him again. This could obviously be rather confusing if an alehouse keeper moved around a lot. This practice died out in the eighteenth century.

Religion was a very early influence on the choosing of names for hostelries and their resulting pub signs. Some of these names date from medieval times. The Crosse Keys, for example, in Gracechurch Street, EC3 refers to the symbol for St Peter who, so the story says, was accorded by Jesus with the guardianship of the keys to Heaven. All the major saints had their symbols hundreds of years ago and they would have been instantly identifiable by almost everyone. The Seven Stars in Carey Street, WC2, one of London's most eccentric pubs, may refer to the seven stars often depicted in ecclesiastical art surrounding the head of the Virgin Mary. It could however refer to those planets that were known in medieval times. The Lamb & Flag, Rose Street, WC2 is a symbol of Christ's Passion. The Salutation, Hammersmith, W6, refers to the Annunciation when the Archangel Gabriel supposedly greeted the Virgin Mary and told her she was pregnant. The Jerusalem, Britton Street, EC1, a successful modern pastiche of an eighteenth century London tavern, shows the severed head of St John the Baptist on its platter. This was demanded by the sinuous Salome after she had danced before the besotted Herod who promised her anything she wanted. She took advice and got what she was told to ask for. St John the Baptist just happened to be in the wrong place at the wrong time.

Signs depicting royalty are common. Sometimes the sign displays a portrait or on other occasions a symbol, often taken from the heraldic charge of the monarch concerned. There is any number of King's Heads, some attempting to show a specific monarch, others simply stylised. The Victoria, W2, shows Queen Victoria, a common subject for a pub name. King & Queen, W1, is an uncommon name and the King's Head & Eight Bells, SW3, was unique, almost certainly gaining this name from the amalgamation of two pubs with the respective names. There are many White Swan and White Horse pubs in London. The first was a device on the badge of Henry IV, Edward III and Edward IV while the latter was associated with Henry VI. Another common sign, the Red Lion, usually derives from the badge of John of Gaunt, a younger son of Edward III. The numerous pubs called the George, are more likely to be a shortening of George & Dragon than a celebration of the Hanoverian Kings George the First to the Fourth, none of whom were popular with the possible exception of George III. Rose & Crown is one of the UK's most common names and is generally taken as a celebration of the coming together of Houses of York and Lancaster consequent on the marriage of Henry VII to Elizabeth of York. There is an example in Stoke Newington, N16. Stratford, E15, has the unusual King Edward VII.

Large numbers of signs commemorate transport and communication in all its various forms. The Running Footman, W1, has a sign declaring that, "I am the only Running Footman." This is true; the name is unique. The Viaduct, Newgate Street, EC1 is a rather fine Victorian pub the name of which commemorates the opening in 1869 of the nearby Holborn Viaduct which joined the City to the West End by a solid viaduct over the valley of the River Fleet. The Doric Arch, NW1 refers of course to the portico designed by Philip Hardwicke to stand in front of Euston Station, the oldest of London's main line termini. It was erected in 1838 and controversially demolished to make way for the rebuilding of the station in the early 1960s. The arch did not entirely die in vain. It alerted the world to the barbarians and vandals masquerading as architects and town planners who, if they had had their way, would have gone on to demolish St Pancras and Kings Cross stations as well. The Narrow Boat, N1, stands in Islington by the Regents Canal and refers to the specialised canal boats that made their way slowly through this part of London. The Railway Tavern, Carshalton, is a neat little pub typical of many that were built close to railway stations in the Greater London suburbs. The Coach & Horses at Kew Green has a name recalling the romance of the stagecoach era. The Cutty Sark, Greenwich, SE10, is less than a stone's throw from the ship of that name in its dry dock. She was built in 1869 on Clydeside and was still in commercial use in 1922, perhaps the most famous of all the tea clippers.

London may not have been the hub of the heavy industries such as iron and steel-making and shipbuilding on which Britain's economic pre-eminence was once based. However, she was the centre of a multiplicity of diverse industrial activities and occupations as befitted one of the most complex and largest cities in the world. The Skinners Arms, Judd Street, WC1 refers to the Skinners Company, one of the City Livery Companies. Established in 1327, they controlled the fur trade. They became rich and influential because for centuries furs were so expensive they could only be afforded by the affluent who loved to strut around in furs as evidence of their conspicuous consumption. In Borough Market, SE1 stands very appropriately the Market Porter. Close by is the more recently opened Barrow Boy and Banker, a name whose irony will not be lost in the Credit Crunch. The Waterman's Arms, Richmond-on-Thames recalls the men who plied their trade ferrying people along or across the Thames, the predecessors of the London cabbies, men who were opposed to the building of London's bridges because they feared it would rob of them of their livings. The familiar Elephant & Castle, SE1 is a device taken from the arms of the Cutlers' Company. The Leather Exchange, SE1, is a reminder that Bermondsey was the major leather-working quarter of London.

London has always been the centre of England's cultural life and a host of pub signs reflect this. Nell of Old Drury, WC2, refers to Nell Gwynne who, when she

The unusual sign of a uniquely-named pub.

wasn't selling oranges, made her name on the stage as a comedienne and then caught the eternally roving eye of Charles II. The pub is close to the Royal Opera House. The Charles Dickens in Southwark is near where Dickens lived while his father was in the Marshalsea Prison for debt. The Richmal Crompton in Bromley is uniquely named after the authoress of the delightful books about William Brown He is a snub-nosed and intrepid boy whose natural sense of mischief lands him in a series of hilarious adventures in which his main opponents are irascible farmers and gardeners, his narcissistic elder sister Ethel, his overly serious elder brother Robert and a young girl, possessed of a formidably strong will and piercing scream worthy of a banshee, by the name of Violet-Elizabeth Bott. The Samuel Pepys, EC4, remembers a great Londoner whose seventeenth-century diaries give us a vivid account of life in the London of his times. It is fitting that he was a devotee of drinking and drinking places. In Kings Cross Road, WC1, there stands a pub which had the interesting name Pindar of Wakefield. It is now called the Water Rats, a unique name referring to the Grand Order of Water Rats which is a charity run by people in show business. The eponymous 'Water Rat' was the name of a pony belonging to the founder. The Betsey in Farringdon Road, EC1, refers to an immortal Dickensian character, Betsey Trotwood, who is David Copperfield's eccentric aunt and benefactor. Ye Olde Cheshire Cheese in Fleet Street, EC4, is one of London's most famous pubs and despite radical re-building, it gives a good impression of how some of the eighteenth-century taverns must have looked. It has been frequented over the years by such literary luminaries as Alexander Pope, Charles Dickens and Arthur Conan Doyle.

We live today in an insidious culture of so-called 'celebrity'. There are many London pubs named after famous people. History may have been kind to the memory of some of these people and even the 'great and the good' often turn out actually to have had feet of clay. However some of those whose names can be seen on the capital's pub signs certainly left something meaningful behind, possibly rather more significant than what some of today's celebrities will achieve. The Daniel Defoe in Stoke Newington, N16, is close to where Defoe was born in 1660. He was a hosiery worker, a soldier, a satirist, a newspaper owner and columnist, a spy, a writer of fiction and a traveller. There are several Lord Nelsons in Greater London including one in West End Lane, High Barnet. Nelson is arguably Britain's greatest naval hero, a naval strategist of genius and a superb leader of men who was also querulous, petty-minded, vain and egotistical. The Prince Blucher, Twickenham, is the last surviving pub of this name. This Prussian aristocratic field-marshal whose full name was Gebhard Leeberecht von Blucher, Prince of Wahistadt, turned up with his troops at exactly the right time at the Battle of Waterloo, 1815, providing some much needed relief for the Duke of Wellington and then pursuing and harrying the fleeing French soldiers through the night. The Sekforde Arms, E1, recalls the unsung Thomas Sekforde who died in 1588. Sekforde was a highly successful and wealthy Elizabethan lawyer and MP who financed one of his servants, Christopher Saxton, to complete the first ever series of county maps. He also provided money for a book, never completed, intended to identify and list all of England's rivers. Aldborough Road North in Ilford has the Dick Turpin. He was an Essex man whose fame lies in his activity as a highwayman. These robbers have been greatly glamourised and Turpin, like so many of his sort, was an ugly, violent and ruthless thug.

Man has a long-standing and extremely complex relationship with the animal world — he is of course an animal himself. Most of the animals, birds or fish that appear on signs seem to be creatures for which he has some affection or regard. No one, for example, has yet celebrated the staphylococcus in a pub name. Elephant is the unusual name of a long-established pub in Fenchurch Street, EC3. At one time it was called Elephant and Castle. Another quadruped rarely appearing on pub signs is the Camel but a small pub with this name can be found in Globe Road, E2. In Lamb's Conduit Street, WC1, stands the Lamb, a pub full of character and charm. In this case the 'Lamb' concerned is not the woolly kind but William Lamb who built the conduit to provide a water supply and very generously distributed 120 pails to the poor women of the area. The Dove in Broadway Market, E8, commemorates a bird which has been held in high regard by man — and wantonly slaughtered. Christianity often depicts the Holy Ghost in the form of a dove. The Greyhound, Hendon, NW4 refers to a graceful and fleet-footed animal in which people are interested these days largely because of racing and betting but the animal was originally bred as a hunting dog. The Dolphin, Sydenham, SE26, shows a member of the order Cetacea. These creatures are generally liked by humans because they seem to be highly intelligent and to have an affinity with us.

There are several pubs in the London area called the Cricketers. Two examples are at Woodford Green, Redbridge and Addiscombe. The image of a typical idyllic English village is of an ancient church tower embowered in gnarled oak trees complete with cawing rooks, a welcoming, ivy-clad and thatched pub overlooking a green with a duck pond in one corner and a cricket pitch on which, of course, a match is taking place. At one time many of the villages once peripheral to London but now firmly in its thrall were something like this affectionate caricature. The idyll is relived in this pub name. The Dog & Duck, Bateman Street, W1, recalls the sport of duck-shooting and the use of man's best friend as a retriever. The pub itself is tiny but oozing character. The Fox & Hounds is a common name nationwide and London has its examples such as that in Latchmere Road near Clapham Junction SW11. Few 'field sports' or 'blood sports' depending on point of view seem to polarise opinion so sharply as fox-hunting but like it or loath it, it has been a feature of England for centuries and its presence is reflected in the frequency of the pub sign. The game played by men with odd-shaped balls is recalled at the Rugby, WC1 and the ancient game of Pall Mall was remembered in a pub of that name in SW1. If the sign was anything to go by, the game looked almost impossibly difficult as players had to hit a ball along an alley and through a suspended iron ring. Presently in Panton Street SW1, is the Tom Cribb, commemorating a nineteenth century former champion pugilist who had been a landlord of this pub.

It is only to be expected that London would have some very odd pub names. A few are mentioned here. They do not include modern gimmicky ones dreamed up by callow philistines in the marketing industry. The Ship & Shovell, Craven Passage, WC2, is really a rather odd pub because it consists of two bits — one on either side of the passage. Sir Clowdisley Shovell or Shovel (1659-1707) made the extraordinary climb from a ship's servant to the rank of admiral in a distinguished career which ended when, after a successful campaign against the French, he was returning to port and a sudden storm blew his flagship and three other ships onto

A stylish tiled pub sign and brewery advertisement. Stoke Newington High Street, N16.

notorious rocks off the Isles of Scilly. His ship was totally wrecked but Shovell somehow managed to crawl ashore where one of the local women on the beach saw that he had a large emerald ring. She then rather uncharitably murdered him (some say by beating him over the head with a shovel) and stole the ring. Possibly unique in Britain is the Jugged Hare, Vauxhall Bridge Road, SW1. This recalls a method of cookery little used today whereby pieces of meat such as hare are cooked in a jug or jar with simmering liquid. It is a slow process which but one which should ensure that the meat is delightfully tender. Not far away, the unique Speaker in Great Peter Street, SW1, recalls the person who chairs parliamentary proceedings. The pub has a division bell so that MPs can tear themselves away from their pints in order to take part in crucial votes. The Bishop's Finger, Smithfield, EC1, is a rare sign referring to an old-fashioned signpost, correctly called a fingerpost. This is a logo of Shepherd Neame of Faversham, the owners of the house. An alternative and irreverent name for this kind of fingerpost is 'Nun's Delight'.

Some pubs have displayed three-dimensional signs and there is a collection of fine examples of these in the Museum of London, London Wall, EC2. There are also some tiled and carved relief signs to be seen. With the spread of literacy in the nineteenth century, painted and three-dimensional signs dropped out of fashion for a period and many of the large number of new pubs that were being built simply had the names painted on the façade or sometimes carved in a prominent position. As more and more pubs were tied to brewers, the spirit of keen competition meant that the name of the pub increasingly took second place to advertisements for the brewery and its products. Many large, custom-built Victorian pubs had prominent glass gaslights extruding from their façades to attract custom and when these were glowing, pub signs were somewhat superfluous. However fashions come and go and there was a marked revival of interest in painted signboards in the 1930s.

Lastly, although it is not as good as having the original still *in situ* and trading, it is some compensation that several old inns and taverns of the City have given their names to existing streets and courts despite the hostelries themselves having long since gone. Examples are: Bull's Head Passage EC3; Rising Sun Court EC1 and Pope's Head Alley, EC3.

Chapter 10

Riverside Pubs

The Thames, they say, is liquid history. Vast quantities of liquid have been consumed in the many historic pubs along the banks of the Thames as it meanders through Greater London towards the sea. Let us look at a selection of Thameside pubs. All are highly recommended!

Twickenham in Middlesex was an ancient riverside village which, even by the early nineteenth century, contained many opulent mansions, home to men whose source of wealth was to be found in enterprises ten and more miles away in London. The Thames was particularly delightful in the vicinity and speculative builders had begun to take advantage of its location to build upmarket dwellings around the village core. The White Swan, The Riverside, TW9, has a dream site facing Eel Pie Island and is a real case of *rus in urbe*, being only yards from the bustling centre of Twickenham.

The White Cross at Riverside, TW9 has a site to die for, close to Richmond Bridge. It was formerly a hotel and was built on the site of an ancient friary in 1835 as Richmond was starting to become a desirable outer-London suburb. Its closeness to the river has meant that floods can cut it off. For some safely inside, that would be their idea of heaven.

At Isleworth stands the London Apprentice which gained its unique name because it was the resort of jaded apprentices of the City Livery Companies who, when off work and in good weather, would row up the river for a serious bout of convivial roistering in its rural surroundings. It dates back to the fifteenth century and proudly boasts that Henry VIII, Elizabeth I and Charles II stayed there overnight. They wouldn't have got much sleep if the apprentices were there because the young men spent their money so freely that the pub stayed open all night to cater for them.

At Strand-on-the-Green, W4, is the City Barge. London's riverside pubs are a rich crop for lovers of unusual and in many cases, unique signs. The City Barge is unique, deriving its name from the Lord Mayor's barge which was once moored nearby. The original pub building was erected in the late fifteenth century but it was extensively rebuilt in the 1940s after receiving a direct hit from a bomb. An oddity is a 'parliamentary clock'. Few of these have survived but they date back to 1797 when Parliament imposed a tax on glass, including that which protected the dials of clocks. It therefore has an open face.

The Dove at Hammersmith, W6, is an ancient pub oozing with historical associations. Legend tells us that Charles II and Nell Gwynne had amorous trysts in the building before it became a pub while James Thomson (1700-48), one of the pub's regulars, is thought to have composed the lyric of 'Rule, Britannia' while mulling over a pint or two in the bar. William Morris (1834-96) who lived nearby took time off from his political and artistic activities to sink a drink in the Dove and was fond of introducing his friends to the place. The novelist A.P. Herbert (1890-1971) was devoted to the pub and featured it thinly disguised as the Pigeons in *The Water Gypsies*, which is probably his best-loved work.

On Millbank, SW1 stands the imposing Morpeth Arms. The Pimlico district in which it is situated was formerly a low-lying marshy area of wasteland until the 1830s when drainage work took place and building development began. The pub's near-neighbour for several decades was the Millbank Penitentiary, a vast, louring and labyrinthine establishment which had been a revolutionary prison when opened in 1816. It introduced the 'silent' regime where everything was done to prevent the prisoners communicating with each other but this proved disastrous because an unacceptably large number of the luckless inmates were driven mad as a consequence. It closed in 1890 and was pulled down in 1903. Prison officers were among the early regulars at the Morpeth Arms. There are various semi-derelict cellars and tunnels under the pub which some say are connected with the penitentiary. They are supposed to be haunted, possibly by the ghost of a convict who preferred to hang himself rather than face transportation. The Tate Gallery stands on part of the site of the penitentiary and the pub makes a pleasant place to retreat to after a visit.

The Anchor, Bankside, SE1 is an ancient hostelry with many antique features but greatly tarted-up since this part of the South Bank has benefited from the opening of the Globe Theatre and Tate Modern and become a vibrant tourist destination. Traditionally Bankside was a district renowned for being bawdy with innumerable drinking places, brothels known as 'stews' where every sexual proclivity could be catered for and all manner of louche places of entertainment. A pub stood on the site which is thought to have been one of Shakespeare's locals and was also perhaps the inn from which Samuel Pepys safely but with growing gloom watched the city he loved being consumed in the Great Fire of 1666. Dr Johnson (1709-84) worked on his dictionary in a room in the Anchor which was reserved for him by Henry Thrale who owned the adjacent brewery. A ghostly dog is said to inhabit the Anchor.

Wapping is something of a mini-cornucopia for aficionados of pubs with unique names. At No.57, Wapping Wall stands the Prospect of Whitby. It is likely that a pub stood on this site as early as 1520 when it was known as the Devil's Tavern because it was the haunt of dangerous smugglers and river pirates. The successor to this pub was first called the Prospect after a Whitby-registered ship was moored close by. The ship became a landmark and so the pub took on its present name in 1777. Among regulars have been Samuel Pepys, Charles Dickens and the artists James McNeill Whistler (1834-1903) and J.M.W. Turner (1775-1851). At No.62, Wapping High Street, stands the Town of Ramsgate, which once had the more run-of-the-mill name the Red Cow which it has been suggested was a politically incorrect reference to a well-known former barmaid. The present attractive name comes from the practice of fishermen from Ramsgate bringing their catches to Wapping Old Stairs nearby where there was a ready market for fresh fish among those living in the district. Nearby, at the ironically-named Execution Dock, felons such as pirates condemned to death for capital offences on the seas were hanged and their bodies left suspended until three tides had ebbed and flowed over them. They were then taken away for burial. Local resident, the infamous Judge Jeffreys, (1648-89) surely the most consummate judicial bully in British history, is thought often to have sat on the pub's balcony and eaten his dinner with great relish while watching the death agonies of the poor wretches being hanged. (This would actually have been physically impossible). Universally hated, Jeffreys tried to escape in disguise to the Continent from Wapping but was recognised and had to be rescued from a mob who wanted to lynch him. The third uniquely-named pub is the Captain Kidd also in Wapping High Street. It is named after the notorious pirate, William Kidd (c.1645-1701) who was hanged at Execution Dock. The stories about Kidd have him down as a swashbuckling, fearsome and bloodthirsty man when in fact he was more like Captain Pugwash of children's television cartoon fame — an incompetent and inept bungler. At No. 76, Narrow Street, Limehouse stands the Grapes, a long, narrow pub with a rear terrace over the Thames. This terrace was used by artist Rex Whistler to capture river scenes on canvas. The present pub was built around 1720 and was used by Dickens.

On the south bank of the Thames at No.101 Bermondsey Wall East stands the pub now known as the Angel. It is an ancient establishment, originally set up by the monks of the rich and powerful Bermondsey Abbey not far away. It is said that in this pub, Christopher Jones, captain of the 'Mayflower', engaged some of the crew for the famous voyage which took early settlers to North America. Later, the dour and rugged Captain Cook (1728-79) spent his last few nights before setting off in 1768 on the heroic circumnavigation of New Zealand and exploration of the east coast of Australia. This was yet another hostelry frequented by the ubiquitous Samuel Pepys (1633-1703). It is amazing that Pepys ever managed to write up his diary never mind attending to his duties as Secretary of the Admiralty. For a couple of centuries this part of the south bank of the Thames was a teeming labyrinth of warehouses, wharves and sinister alleys and impenetrable slums where a fraternity of highly-skilled criminals made a lucrative living plundering cargoes on the ships, lighters and quaysides of the Pool of London. Now the area, which had been in the doldrums for several decades, is becoming gentrified and the pub, which was becoming structurally unsafe, has been rescued and restored. Looking up river, the pub offers a view of Tower Bridge to die for.

Typical affectionate mocking by Rowlandson.

At No.117, Rotherhithe Street, SE16 can be found the Mayflower. A pub has stood on this site for many centuries and it was originally called the Shippe. The *Mayflower* was moored close by for some time before it set off on the voyage, which eventually took pioneering settlers to establish a colony in North America. The master of the *Mayflower*, Captain Jones returned to Rotherhithe and was buried in the churchyard of nearby St Mary's. An extensive rebuilding took place in the eighteenth century after which the pub was renamed the Spread Eagle and Crown and it only became the Mayflower in 1957 in honour of the voyage of the Pilgrim Fathers. The pub claims to incorporate some of the timbers from the *Mayflower* in its structure and has the rare distinction for a pub of being licensed to sell not only British postage stamps but American ones as well.

The Trafalgar Tavern, Park Row, Greenwich, SE16 is an imposing building erected in the 1830s replacing an ale-house called the George. The Trafalgar was perhaps the most notable of a number of local hostelries which became famous for their 'whitebait suppers'. Greenwich was just far enough out of central London to tempt all manner of its citizens to take a cruise down the river for drinks and whitebait. So tempting was this excursion that on a number of occasions Gladstone and his entire cabinet sailed down to Greenwich on a specially commandeered barge for a beer and whitebait binge. At this time whitebait swam in huge shoals in the Thames from spring to summer. These tiny fish were deep-fried, heavily seasoned with cayenne pepper and sprinkled with lemon juice and regarded by all classes as a great delicacy. Those who could afford it liked their whitebait washed down with champagne. In 1915, the Trafalgar closed as a pub and undertook various roles until reopening as a pub in the 1960s.

Chapter 11

The London Pub in Literature

The pubs of London are cultural signposts and an essential part of its identity. Here we will attempt a brief consideration of the role played by London's pubs in literature, painting and films.

The crucial role of the Tabard in Southwark as the gathering place for the motley group of pilgrims in Chaucer's *Canterbury Tales* has been mentioned elsewhere. Chaucer clearly distinguished between the Tabard as a genteel establishment with some class and the alehouse favoured by his character the Pardoner which was a more earthy place appealing to lovers of the bawdy and boisterous.

Probably the best-known pub in English literature is the Boar's Head Tavern in Eastcheap and perhaps its most famous drinker is Falstaff. They both appear in a number of plays by Shakespeare written in the 1590s. The scene itself is set in the early fifteenth century and it contrasts the simple pleasures and robust good cheer of Falstaff and his world with the increasingly centrifugal influence that government in London was exerting. A tendency to control public behaviour in relation to drinking and drinking places had been evident for two or three centuries but was clearly accelerating at the time Shakespeare was writing. Old informal come-day, go-day practices were increasingly coming under attack from Protestant ideas of sobriety and thrift. A growing number of acts sought to control drinking places and also to tackle the issue of mendicity. There was an implied association between the two. In these plays, tavern life is portrayed as life simply being frittered away. It was inimical to the regular work-discipline required of a nation that we can now see was moving towards the Industrial Revolution. Time and time-keeping were taking on a new urgency. It was a boom time for clockmakers. Falstaff with his slightly dissipated enjoyment of food, drink and fun is likeable but he and his sort essentially belong to the past. In these plays, Shakespeare gives us another memorable character in Mistress Quickly, the stout landlady of the Boar's Head with her unintentional double-entendres. In *Measure for Measure* (1604) Shakespeare alludes to the difficulties of a monarch attempting to sanitise and control the brothels and bawdy taverns of a city which is London in all but name.

Thomas Dekker (?1570-1632) was born in London, spent much of his life there and reflects its daily life and mores vividly in his writings. In 'Lantern and Candlelight' (1608), a messenger is sent from Hell to London to find people he could bring back with him when he returns. He is directed to taverns where he will find 'prodigals' and to ordinaries to dine with 'silken fools'. Also in ordinaries will be found those predatory rogues known as 'Gull-Gropers' who 'befriended' callow young men from the provinces who had just arrived in London, the better to dupe them later. In the 'Wonderful Year' (1603) when London was hit by a serious outbreak of the plague, we have a drunkard coming out of an alehouse in the dark and falling into a pit full of bodies which the sexton has failed to cover over. The drunkard's initial thoughts as he lies there, befuddled, are that the people around him are his drinking companions. Dekker's London drinking houses shed a malign shadow.

In the seventeenth century, the incipient conflict between the old land-owning aristocracy and the rising industrial and mercantile bourgeoisie came to a head in the Civil War. Pubs, drinking and general joie de vivre were associated with the King's supporters and ascetic, stern denial of the sensuous pleasures was associated with the Parliamentarians. In so far as Parliament's supporters drank at all, their beverage was beer and it was drunk in alehouses. Those supporting the King drank in taverns where they tippled wine with a sense of superiority.

Samuel Pepys (1633-1703) began to write his famous diary in 1660, the year when Charles II was restored to the throne amidst widespread rejoicing from a populace tired of the censorious activities of the puritans. Not only do these diaries provide fascinating insights into the social life of London in the ten years during which he put pen to paper, but they also provide evidence of his own inner tensions. These involved his love of taverns and theatres which he was constantly trying to keep in check to ensure that they did not obstruct the progress of his career. He was also subject to much heart-searching because he had been brought up in a Puritan family. References to inns, taverns, alehouses, ordinaries and theatres lace Pepys's Diaries. He drank first thing in the morning, sporadically during the day and often with some single-minded devotion in the evening. It is perfectly clear that he found attendance in these places crucial to his professional and personal lives. Some excerpts from his diary follow:

On 9 February 1660 he complains of a bad head as a result of a hangover. He was rather preoccupied by his health. He had painful kidney stones removed on 26 March 1658 and he celebrated the relief gained by getting seriously drunk every year on the anniversary. He seems obsessed with the damage that drinking is doing to his body and yet his ambition to be at the centre of life in London involves what would now be called 'networking', most of which involved drinking in public. On 9 August 1660 he varied his normal activity when he allows himself to be accompanied by his wife, in this case to The Leg, in King Street. This was most unusual since he used drinking places to watch and make lewd proposals to any likely women he found in such places. The entry for 22 September 1660 makes a candid admission while not attempting to excuse his behaviour. 'To Westminster to my Lord's; and there...

vomited up all my breakfast, my stomach being ill all this day by reason of the last night's debauch'. On 14 November 1660 Pepys reveals his love of tavern life when he described a session in the Dolphin including, 'there we did drink a great quantity of Sack. And did tell many merry stories, and in good humours were we all'. He constantly swears to give up wine and congratulates himself on 'only' drinking ale and beer but sooner or later, he succumbs to temptation and gets drunk on wine again. He generally approved of ordinaries except on 25 April 1661 when, 'At noon Mr Moore and I went to an ordinary at the King's Head in Tower Street and there had a dirty dinner'. In August 1663 the poor man has once more abjured wine and in his rush to be abstemious has eaten nothing and only drunk small beer. The result: 'I am so mightily troubled with wind that I know not what to do almost'.

Pepys was something of a trencherman and he describes in detail a meal he enjoyed at the Bell, King Street, Westminster. It consisted of roast leg of veal, bacon, two capons, sausages and fritters. What we would now called 'pub-meals' feature frequently in his Diary. He has bloaters at the Dolphin in Tower Street, a place he mentions no fewer than forty-five times. At the Royal Oak in Lombard Street, he eagerly consumed chine of beef with a dish of marrow bones. At the King's Head, Bow, in 18 August 1662, he ate 'a breakfast of eggs'. On 15 September 1660, Pepys had bought a piece of salmon and he repaired to the Sun in New Fish Street in the City in order to eat it.

Among his lovers was Mrs Lane and on 15 August 1664 he tells of going to the Trumpett where, 'I had my pleasure with her'. On 15 December 1664 an entry makes it clear that he was engaged in fruitlessly cruising around various lowlife alehouses looking for sex. On 2 September 1666 Pepys gave the world his famous description of the Great Fire. At the time he was in an alehouse on Bankside. As the diary goes on it is evident it is the drinking place which increasingly provides the theatre for his sexual activities although occasionally he is frustrated at not being able to lay his hands on a bed. Such a mishap occurs at the Dog Tavern where he meets Mrs Martin on 18 February 1668. Pepys gave up writing his diary in 1669 because of his concerns that he was losing his eyesight.

Ned Ward (1667-1731) is off the radar as far as most literary critics are concerned. Ward was the genial host of the King's Head Tavern and a journalistic hack. In 1698 he began a series of monthly instalments called 'The London Spy' in which he ostensibly moralised on the vanities and vices of the London citizenry while doing so in graphic detail and with evident prurient relish. His writing is journalistic and unashamedly aimed at the popular market. As a tavern-keeper he was well placed to observe human foibles close to hand and he has the skill of giving his readers the impression that he himself is a participant in the low-life scenes he describes. His discourse is in the form of a narration by a visitor to London whose friends show him the sights. His first experience of a London tavern is when he is taken to an ordinary and meets his friend's shady companions who include a counterfeiter, a highwayman, a pimp and a crooked gambler. They eat, they drink toasts and they become uproariously drunk. He is impressed by their swearing and with the kind of delightful metaphor of which he is capable: 'Oaths were as plenty as weeds in an almshouse garden'. In the evening they repair to another tavern where they drink, exchange witticisms and are joined by some young ladies. Ward does not give the impression that the presence of women is particularly unusual nor that they are there simply for sexual purposes. In the second episode, he and his companion, who is a physician who numbers syphilitic prostitutes among his patients, visit a louche coffee house which doubles as a brothel and then patronise an ill-lit but boisterous establishment close to the Thames used by disreputable people having business on the river. This is part-alehouse and part doss-house. Space precludes us from following Ward and his companion on all their peregrinations. 'The London Spy' does not flow easily for the modern reader but it gives us some idea of the place of the drinking house in the popular culture and general social life of London at the end of the seventeenth century.

'The Beggar's Opera' by John Gay, produced in 1728, was enormously popular at the time. It contains characters drawn from contemporary London life such as Captain Macheath, the likeably roguish highwayman, Peachum the receiver of stolen goods and thief-taker and Lockit, the Newgate warder on the make. The tavern is presented as a natural and congenial place in which people of this sort meet and socialise. They are by no means among the poorer elements of London society. However, the tavern soon proves to be a perfidious location because it is where Macheath is turned over to Peachum and the authorities by the very people with whom he resorts.

Charles Dickens (1812-70) was a Londoner by adoption and seemingly also by temperament and in his voluminous writings he manages to get under the skin of the metropolis like no other writer of his time. Hostelries of every kind abound, many of them in London and while Dickens portrays some of them in bleak colours, he seems generally to understand and appreciate the central role they played in the life of the capital. In *Pickwick Papers* (1836-7), he gives us this highly descriptive passage:

In the Borough, especially, there still remain some half dozen inns, which have preserved their external features unchanged, and which have escaped alike the rage for public improvement, and the encroachment of private speculation. Great, rambling, queer, old places they are, with galleries, and passages, and staircases, wide enough and antiquated enough to furnish materials for a hundred ghost stories...

In *Dombey and Son* (1847-8,) we are presented with the perfect inn, the Saracen's Head in which:

The candles were brought, the fire was stirred up, and a fresh log of wood was thrown on. In ten minutes' time, a waiter was laying the cloth for dinner, the curtains were drawn, the fire was blazing brightly, and everything looked as if the travellers had been expected, and their comforts prepared, for days beforehand.

By contrast we have a symbol of the rapid superseding of the coaching inns by the all-conquering railway: 'A brand-new tavern, redolent of fresh mortar and size, and fronting nothing at all, had taken for its sign the Railway Arms'. The Boot is the meeting place of the rioters in *Barnaby Rudge* (1841) and the Maypole also plays a major role as a location in the story. The reader is treated to a lengthy description of the building, of its landlord and of some of its regulars. Although a village pub, it was close enough to London to be within its thrall. A number of low drinking places feature in *Oliver Twist* (1837-9). In *Sketches by Boz* (1836-7), Dickens reveals his sympathy for the underdog in his description of a gin palace and he adds:

> Gin-drinking is a great vice in England, but poverty is a greater; and until you can cure it, or persuade a half-famished wretch not to seek relief in the temporary oblivion of his own misery…gin-shops will increase in number and splendour.

Arthur Morrison (1863-1945) was a minor writer who produced a number of socially realistic novels about working-class life in the East End of London, the best known of which was probably *The Child of the Jago* (1896). Drink and pubs feature in Morrison's bleak stories and he seems to have less sympathy than Dickens for the vices of London's inhabitants. For him, they seem to be as much to blame for their blighted lives as does the economic and social system which grinds them down. Jack London (1876-1916) In *The People of the Abyss* (1903), this American writer relates the experiences of several weeks spent living in the slums of the East End. In his opinion the ubiquitous pubs had a debilitating effect on the lives of the local people and their desire to make something of their lives.

London pubs feature in innumerable films, even if only playing a minor role as background in a street scene. They are too numerous to list so examples from two districts only will have to suffice.

SOHO, W1

The Three Horseshoes, Green Street, *Bend It Like Beckham* (2002); The Spice of Life, Moor Street; *Sid and Nancy* (1986); Duke's Bar, Old Compton Street; *Wonderland* (1994) and The Dragon, Gerrard Street, *Agent Cody Banks 2* (2004).

BOROUGH, SE1

The Market Porter, Stoney Street, *The Young Americans* (1993), *Hard Men* (1996), *Keep the Aspidistra Flying* (1997); The Globe, Bedale Street, *Pool of London* (1952), *Blue Ice* (1992), *Lassiter* (1986) and the George Inn, Borough High Street, *Tom Brown's Schooldays* (1950).

Chapter 12

Some Historic London Pubs

The author decided not to try to provide a selection of *typical* London pubs since it is impossible to establish what is 'typical'. He has contented himself therefore with a personal choice listing forty pubs of different sorts which he feels have interesting historical associations, fittings or furnishings or something that marks them out and makes them particularly worth going to. The author has visited all these pubs, in some cases much too often, and believes that they are all pleasant places in which to have a drink, preferably of real ale. Riverside pubs and others described elsewhere are not included. They are listed under postal districts.

E3

WIDOW'S SON, 75, Devons Road, Bow. A famous East End boozer, also known as the 'Bun House'. The story is told that around 1848 the son of the widowed licensee went off to sea and she promised to save him a hot cross bun for his return. He never came back but the pub displays a collection of buns baked annually since that time. There are some interesting internal fittings.

EC1

CROWN, CLERKENWELL GREEN. Situated next to the Green with its proud place in London's radical history, a convivial pub located in an old building which, like so many others in London, has a somewhat contrived but successful feeling of antiquity. Karl Marx is said to have enjoyed a noggin or two in this pub.

The name of an old brewery recorded in a pub window. 'Three Kings', Farringdon Lane, EC1.

FOX & ANCHOR, 115, Charterhouse Street. This has a remarkable art nouveau frontage and unselfconscious pleasantly worn interior. Close to Smithfield Market, this has the advantage for those who can't sleep, of opening at 6.30 in the morning.

OLDE MITRE TAVERN, Ely Place. One of London's most elusive pubs, this ancient building stands on land which was once part of the Bishop of Ely's London town house. The place oozes historic character and displays a piece of a cherry tree said to have come from a maypole around which Elizabeth I cavorted. This pub with its oak panelling and beams gives a good imitation of an eighteenth century tavern.

THREE KINGS, 7, Clerkenwell Close. Eccentric exterior signage and eccentric items are on display inside the pub which has remained reassuringly down-to-earth in this gentrifying district.

VIADUCT TAVERN, 126, Newgate Street. Standing opposite the Old Bailey, this pub takes its name from the nearby Holborn Viaduct. Remnants of its Victorian fittings can be seen including 'soft porn' murals.

EC2

THE OLD DR BUTLER'S HEAD, Mason's Avenue, Coleman Street. Tucked away near the Guildhall and taking some finding, this pub is not as old as its appearance suggests but manages to look and feel like an old City tavern and chop-house. Dr Butler was a seventeenth century quack doctor.

EC3

HOOP & GRAPES, 47, Aldgate High Street. The only surviving genuine old timber-framed building in the City, this ancient hostelry somehow managed to survive the Great Fire of 1666. Extensively rebuilt and refurbished but it has the typical 'old-world' style of so many City watering holes.

EC4

BLACKFRIAR, 174 Queen Victoria Street. This is one of the most extraordinary pubs in London and possibly in the UK. Built in 1875, it is shaped like a wedge of cheese. Early in the 1900s, the ground floor was remodelled by a follower of the Arts and Crafts Movement around a 'Merrie England' theme. The interior contains a riot of variegated polished marble, alabaster figures and copper or bronze relief panels showing jolly-looking, rotund friars. Some of the reliefs are the work of a sculptor of national repute, Henry Poole, R.A. Outside above the main door the pub sign is the carved figure of an extremely stout, benevolent friar. There are also various bas-relief carvings, some by Poole and the pub's name picked out in mosaic. A not-to-be-missed pub.

Art nouveau lettering on exterior of Black Friar pub.

PUNCH TAVERN, 99, Fleet Street. An extremely ornate, even extravagant pub with glittering mirrors, etched glass and fine faience tilework. This is supposedly where *Punch Magazine*, was originally thought of. Like many of the other fine hostelries along Fleet Street, it has had a slightly listless air since the newspapers that made the street world-famous and the journalists and printers who slaked their thirsts so greedily, were relocated.

N1

ISLAND QUEEN, 87, Noel Road. The author has a liking for eccentric pubs and this one in its quiet way fits the description, having what can only be described as a vaguely piratical theme. It also has some good surviving old fittings and is in an attractively quiet part of Islington away from the hurly-burly around the Angel.

KING'S HEAD, Upper Street. This enormous pub incorporating a theatre has risen with the social rise of Islington over the last twenty years. The place is a bit scruffy, a bit bohemian and definitely more than a bit eccentric because it still prices are still in pre-decimal money rung up in a till every bit as old as Methusalah.

WENLOCK ARMS, 26, Wenlock Road. The Wenlock Arms is a modest street corner London alehouse typical of hundreds of similar establishments of which so many have disappeared or changed out of all recognition. It may look modest and unassuming and be in a fairly nondescript area but it is revered among devotees of real ale.

NW1

QUINN'S, 65, Kentish Town Road. Almost garish on the outside, this pub is that rare item in London, a genuine Irish pub that does not have to resort to having a silly name or being decorated internally with a job-lot of mock-Irish tat just to prove how authentic it is. It benefits from having been in the same family for approaching twenty years.

A reminder that Hampstead once set out its stall to be a spa.

NW3

FLASK, 14, Flask Walk, Hampstead. The name is a reminder that wells around Hampstead were once believed to have medicinal properties, the water being bottled for sale. Hampstead was and is a village, close enough to central London to make it a place of desirable residence and of popular recreation. The present building dates from 1874 and unusually these days, has a clear demarcation between the saloon and public bar areas.

HOLLY BUSH, 22, Holly Mount, Hampstead. The village has always attracted artists and literati and George Romney and John Constable are likely to have dropped in for a pint or two. Hampstead has a character both bourgeois and proletarian and this relaxed pub with its curious internal fittings and layout fits that bill perfectly.

SPANIARDS, Spaniards Road, Hampstead. Situated on the Heath, *The Spaniards* has a suitably worn feeling and oozes historical character, something that grows organically and cannot be artificially installed by purblind interior designers employed by a pubco. Its unique name is the subject of speculation as are is its supposed connections with Dick Turpin who spent so much time in pubs, it's a wonder how he ever got round to any highway robbery.

WASHINGTON, 50, England's Lane, Primrose Hill. An imposing if somewhat spartan exterior hides an interior with a wealth of some of the best original Victorian fittings to be found in a London pub. This pub has been refurbished to attract the conspicuous spenders of this fashionable area of the Metropolis — see your bank manager before you go!

SE1

ANCHOR TAP, 23, Horsleydown Road. Adjacent to the former Anchor Brewery, closed by Courage in the 1980s, and to the iconic Tower Bridge, this beautifully preserved old pub still provides a hint or two that it was once the resort of tarry sailors and horny-handed stevedores from the wharves and warehouses of the Pool of London.

GEORGE INN, 77, Borough High Street. This remarkable survivor is mentioned in all the guide books and so has become something of a cliché. An inn stood on this site in the sixteenth century, most of which was consumed in the great Southwark fire of 1676. It was rebuilt and became an important inn servicing coaches and waggons, the only one left in London with the ancient open galleries characteristic of its kind. Just one wing of the original three survives but the remnant is delightful, inside and out. Fortunately, it is owned by the National Trust and it is an ancient monument of outstanding importance.

SE10

RICHARD I, 52-54, Royal Hill, Greenwich. Often known as 'Tolly's' because for many years it was a rare London outlet for Tolly Cobbold, the Ipswich brewers, this is a narrow, well-worn and welcoming establishment handy for all local attractions. Greenwich is a village with extraordinary contrasts of gentility with aged, serene and extremely expensive housing, some modern buildings of quite extraordinary ugliness and a share of urban menace.

SE21

CROWN & GREYHOUND, 73, Dulwich Village. It is trite but a truism to say that London is an agglomeration of villages and Dulwich manages to keep such a feeling more than most. The centre of the village is dominated by this enormous pub, a grandiloquent combining of two existing pubs which was created about 1900 on the no-expenses-spared basis popular at that time in London pub circles.

SW1

GRENADIER, 18, Wilton Row, Belgravia. Tucked away behind some of the most expensive real estate in the world, this small pub has a resident ghost and, uniquely, a sentry box outside and a notice stating that only those customers who have arrived by taxi or on foot will be served. The pub was originally the officers' mess for the nearby barracks. People come long distances on Sundays to sample the famous Bloody Marys.

SW12

NIGHTINGALE, 97, Nightingale Lane, Balham. This district was mostly wooded countryside until it was sold off for fairly exclusive housing development around 1870. The pub dates from the 1870s and was designed to look rather rustic and very unlike most of the pubs that were being erected around London at that time. It is friendly, unassuming and a haven for people from all classes. Over the years, the regulars have raised money to pay for the training of more than thirty guide dogs.

SW18

CAT'S BACK, 86, Point Pleasant, Wandsworth. There was a pub on this site since 1865 called 'Ye Old House at Home'. It was an honest-to-goodness old-fashioned working class boozer which has been revamped as an eccentric, rather bohemian and relaxed pub full of eclectic clutter which somehow manages not to look contrived.

SPREAD EAGLE, 71, Wandsworth High Street. By any standards, this is a grand pub, rebuilt in about 1898 at the peak of the craze for ebullient large, richly-furnished and fitted pubs which made a statement by dominating their surroundings. It stood opposite the late-lamented Young's Brewery which had seemed as timeless and secure as the Rock of Gibraltar.

W1

DUKE OF WELLINGTON, 94A, Crawford Street. This pub is a shrine to the memory of the 'Iron Duke', one of England's greatest military leaders. It would be wrong to say that you can't get in the door for Wellington memorabilia but the place is a wall-to-wall museum of items related, no matter how tenuously, to the old military warhorse. This is a deeply eccentric pub.

STAR & GARTER, 62, Poland Street. It would be churlish not to include a Soho pub because it has several well worth visiting. Soho gives the odd impression of somehow being at the centre of things yet also being a village and lacking many of the intimidating huge buildings found elsewhere. This is a small but bustling, cheerful and totally unpretentious and old-fashioned boozer.

W2

VICTORIA, 10A, Strathearn Place. Located near to Paddington station in an area sometimes called Tyburnia from being close to Tyburn, London's major place of execution, this pub is elegant both inside and out. Many of its fine mirrors, mahogany woodwork and other fittings date from the mid-1860's, a rare date in London these days and although the interior has been opened out, it is still very stylish.

W4

TABARD, Bath Road, Turnham Green. This very stylish pub was designed by Richard Norman Shaw, an architect of national repute, in 1880, as a watering hole for the exclusive residential development known as Bedford Park. The pub was intended to conform with the Arts & Craft Movement influence which was so evident in nearby Bedford Park and it has kept some of the fine fittings and furnishings from that time.

W8

CHURCHILL ARMS, 119, Kensington Church Street. No one could describe this pub as understated. In the summer months it almost disappears from sight behind a display of flowers and foliage of prodigious proportions. Many pubs have a theme — some would call them gimmicks. This pub has several themes — chamber pots and Churchill — there may be a loose connection; hat boxes and butterflies. It features highly in the author's list of eccentric London pubs.

UXBRIDGE ARMS, 13, Uxbridge Street. Tucked coyly away not far from the previous and the succeeding pubs, this small back-street house has — praise be! — avoided the temptation to change its formula. It is just a simple, warm and welcoming local with no gimmicks and no need to pander to the Notting Hill set. It is so good because it keeps it simple.

WINDSOR CASTLE, 114, Campden Hill Road, W11. 'Rus in urbe', the country in the town, is a concept which appeals to the average English person. It is therefore a delight to come across a pub exuding such a feeling in an unequivocally urban setting only two minute's walk from Notting Hill Gate. A glorious profusion of hanging baskets on the outside is a delightful preparation for a simple and relatively modern interior featuring a lot of slightly knocked-about and comfortable woodwork. Plush this pub is not nor, hopefully, will it ever be but is friendly, relaxed and welcoming.

W9

WARRINGTON HOTEL, 93, Warrington Crescent. Maida Vale. This vastly imposing stuccoed pub is a rebuilding in the 1890s of an earlier pub on the same site. Recently expensively refurbished, the fittings and furnishings are impressive and worth examining but perhaps it is the sheer audacious scale of the place which is the biggest source of wonderment. This is the archetype of the Victorian 'gin palace'.

WC1

CITTIE OF YORK, 22, High Holborn. High on the list of London's eccentric hostelries, this pub is a phantasmagoria of eclectic and historically inaccurate interior design concepts, created in the 1920s. One theme is 'Olde English' with a kind of baronial hall of a sort never seen in reality as the main drinking space. There is much handsome woodwork, long rows of capacious vats over the bars and there are several extremely unusual carrels or booths for those who want to withdraw from the throng. It is somehow typical of this extraordinary building that the huge stove dating back to the early nineteenth century has a flue going downwards.

A typically well-built, even stylish pub built to serve a neighbourhood close to Waterloo Station.

LAMB, 94, Lamb's Conduit Street, Bloomsbury. This would be the pub of choice to be marooned in for a week or the place to have one's ashes scattered. The building dates from 1729 but its fittings are more recent. They include splendid snob screens. A music-player predating the juke box is on display. It is known as a 'Polyphon' and it can be played in return for a contribution to charity. This is a bustling, cosmopolitan pub with a delightfully 'chilled-out air', probably the author's favourite in London.

PRINCESS LOUISE, 208, High Holborn. On balance, this probably possesses the finest interior of any pub in London. It is large, opulent and contains craftsmanship of absolutely the highest quality. Recent renovations by the owners, Samuel Smith's of Tadcaster, have been highly sympathetic as indeed they have been with most of their London pub estate. A ceiling of lyncrusta is complemented by a wealth of tiles and wall mirrors. It would be an insult to the pub to visit it and not use the men's urinal, as fine a repository for fluid excretions as could be found anywhere. If you want to see how the Victorians upgraded their pubs in the 1890s, look no further.

WC2

SALISBURY, 90, St Martin's Lane, Covent Garden. The name celebrates Lord Salisbury, the wily old late-Victorian politician who frequently rode to work on a tricycle. This pub was upgraded in the great pub rebuilding boom of the late 1890s and it has an exuberant interior with superb glasswork, an original island bar counter and numerous art nouveau bronze statuettes. Situated in the heart of Theatreland, it can get extremely busy.

SEVEN STARS, 53, Carey Street. An old small, well-worn and well-loved pub close to the Royal Courts of Justice and with legal eagles well to the fore among its clientele, this is another of London's eccentric pubs. Any pub which has a landlady by the name of Roxy Beaujolais and a cat of commanding presence called Tom Paine, has to be worth visiting. Fascinating old posters line the walls. Interesting food.

SHERLOCK HOLMES, 10-11, Northumberland Street. If a pub has to have a gimmick, then it ought to be a good one as indeed it is with this pub. It is strange to think of a pub festooned from floor to ceiling with the memorabilia of someone who never existed. However, Sherlock Holmes is one of English literature's most enduring creations and devoted pilgrims make their way from across the world make their way here to revel in what is basically a pub full of tat. You don't have to be a Sherlock Holmes fan to enjoy it.

Also available from Amberley Publishing

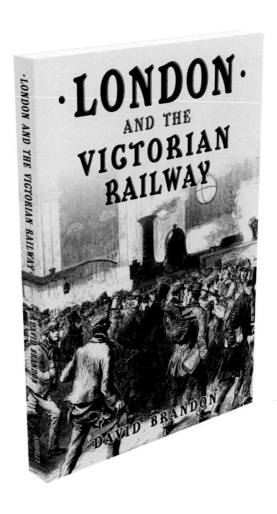

London and the
Victorian Railway
David Brandon

ISBN 978-1-84868-228-3
£14.99

Also available from Amberley Publishing

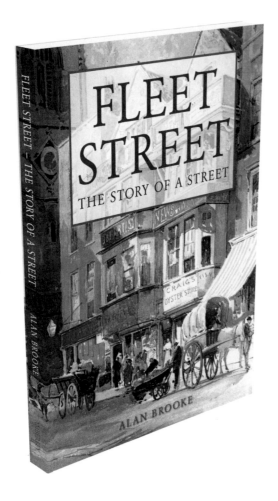

Fleet Street
The Story of a Street
Alan Brooke

ISBN 978-1-84868-229-0
£12.99

Available from all good bookshops or order direct
from our website www.amberleybooks.com